Praise for *Dear Jay, Love Dad*

"We all have much to learn from the loving, encouraging, and insightful letters of Bud Wilkinson to his son. While Bud was undoubtedly a gifted football coach, these letters show that his success was deeply rooted in his personal values and in his love for young people."
—David Boren, President of the University of Oklahoma

"Jay Wilkinson has done what many a son has wished he could do for his father—create a loving and revealing look at the man who has had such a deeply positive influence on his life."
—Charlie Rose, broadcast journalist and host of *Charlie Rose*

"Bud Wilkinson's success as a coach was due not just to the speed, strength, and skill of his players but also to the values and principles that guided every action he took and every decision he made. Those values and principles, articulated in these letters, can inspire leaders today to achieve success—whether in business, politics, or academia—with integrity."
—Roy Bostock, Chairman of the Board of Yahoo! Inc.

"The life Jay Wilkinson describes in this wonderful book is the life of faith. He may not have intended to do that, but faith runs through all of these letters like a golden thread. Jay helps make our own faith come alive in these words of a father to his son."
—Right Reverend Steven Charleston, Interim Dean,
St. Paul's Cathedral, Oklahoma City

Dear Jay,

Love Dad

Friday

Dear Jay —

It was good to talk to you — I know things will get better because you are the kind of person who can adjust & find the good in all situations.

When I read your letter, I recalled vividly many similar times in my life. When I left home to go to Shattuck, I was truly blue. Yet I know now how fine a thing it was for me & my future. The training I received has made my life good. When I left you, Pat, & Mother to go to sea during the war, I was really shaken. I loved you & wanted to watch you & help you as you grew up — & I was leaving not knowing if I'd ever get back again. But once more, the experience & training I received more than compensated for the heartaches. Then too, I had the personal satisfaction of knowing I had done my duty.

One of the first things an education brings to people is the realization that the world is a big place — full of many different ideas & ways of doing things. You have watched our team practice & team. You're that kind of person too, and I will prepare yourself to do bigger & better things when you,

Always remember that I believe in you no matter what. You must do what seems right to you. Don't ever be swayed by what "other people will think." My Grandmother, a great lady — one of the finest I've ever known — always told me when I was a young

stand alone ... ful living.
... ways do
... good judgment
... because you
... think you should do"

... etter yesterday before
... turday. Norman tried
... y miss their "Big Tiger"

defense — as well as offense.

I love you, Jay, more than anything in life. Don't worry about things — live each day by doing your best. Will look forward to talking to you tomorrow.

Love always,
Dad

quite natural
Bill Murray
wondering
what they do
the job do

situation
of how
facing
Challe
have
I ha
o
on
love Duke — to

Dear Jay,

Love Dad

Bud Wilkinson's Letters
to His Son

Jay Wilkinson

Foreword by Mike Krzyzewski

UNIVERSITY OF OKLAHOMA PRESS : NORMAN

Also by Jay Wilkinson

(with Gretchen Hirsch) *Bud Wilkinson: An Intimate Portrait of an American Legend* (Urbana, Ill., 1994)

This book is published with the generous assistance of the Wallace C. Thompson Endowment Fund, University of Oklahoma Foundation.

Library of Congress Cataloging-in-Publication Data

Wilkinson, Jay.
Dear Jay, love dad : Bud Wilkinson's letters to his son / Jay Wilkinson.
    p.   cm.
ISBN 978-0-8061-4247-0 (hardcover : alk. paper)
1 Wilkinson, Bud, 1916–1994—Correspondence. 2. Football coaches—United States—Biography. 3. Oklahoma Sooners (Football team)—History. 4. University of Oklahoma—Football—History. I. Title.
GV939.W48A3 2012
796.332092—dc23
[B]
2011029289

The paper in this book meets the guidelines for permanence and durability of the Committee on Production Guidelines for Book Longevity of the Council on Library Resources, Inc. ∞

1 2 3 4 5 6 7 8 9 10

To Mary Shifflett Wilkinson,

my mother

Contents

Illustrations

Photographs are from the author's collection unless otherwise indicated in the caption.

Foreword

Two is better than one only if two can act as one. Over the last thirty-seven years as a head coach I have told my players that for them to reach their full potential, we must act as one, player and coach. Neither of us can do it alone. But, when we do act as one, some truly amazing things can happen.

Coach Bud Wilkinson understood this concept better than anyone who has ever coached. His remarkable record is proof. In *Dear Jay, Love Dad*, we are able to take an intimate look at how Coach Wilkinson developed this relationship with his son through a series of remarkable letters written during Jay's undergraduate and graduate years of college.

To develop this special relationship, it is essential that certain things occur. You must be able to communicate in a truthful manner. No lies. Ever! As a result of this truthful communication, trust is developed. You must also care for each other and develop collective responsibility. In other words, you win and you lose together. A bond is formed. You then feel a great sense of pride knowing you are a team.

Imagine receiving letters from your parent filled with guidance, encouragement, and love while you are learning and becoming an adult—knowing each day that someone believes in you and is there to help you. It is positive learning at its best.

I love the manner in which Coach Wilkinson explained his philosophy of life. He was able to teach and not preach lessons on a value-based life. He knew that when these lessons were embraced by his son, they would lead to success and happiness. It seems so simple: "Do what is right and be confident enough to follow your instincts. I will always be there for you." Coach Wilkinson was.

For Jay to share these treasured letters with all of us is a remarkable gift. Thank you, Jay, and thank you, Coach Wilkinson. Both of you became one!

> Mike Krzyzewski
> Head Basketball Coach,
> Duke University

Preface

Not long ago I delivered a keynote address at the official naming of a room in my father's honor at the Oklahoma Sports Hall of Fame building in Oklahoma City. During that talk, to convey new perspectives and insights about him, I read from one of the letters he had written to me while I was in graduate school.

Some people today may not remember him, but there are few coaches, in any sport, who have been more celebrated and honored than Bud Wilkinson. Over a seventeen-year period his University of Oklahoma football teams won fourteen conference titles and three national championships and orchestrated win streaks of thirty-one and forty-seven straight college football games; the latter mark remains a National Collegiate Athletic Association (NCAA) record more than half a century later. Equally important is that during that time almost 90 percent of his players graduated, and his teams were known for conducting themselves as gentlemen both on and off the field. Through his leadership he instilled pride, self-esteem, and enthusiasm in the people of Oklahoma. In all aspects of his life, he commanded admiration and respect.

After that keynote address, I decided to go back and read the forty-seven letters he had sent me while I was in college and graduate school. Several additional letters had been either misplaced or lost in the ensuing years. These letters were written over a six-year period between 1960 and 1966 against the backdrop of such historical events as the televised presidential debates between John Kennedy and Richard Nixon and the buildup to the Vietnam War. During that period America experienced great tragedy, turmoil, and social change, including the assassination of President Kennedy, bloody civil rights demonstrations, and the passage of the Civil Rights Act of 1964.

As I studied their contents, I realized the letters provided remarkable insights into themes as vital and relevant today as when the words were written fifty years ago. My father affirmed that life is ever changing and will continue to be so, but the great truths remain. The principles in his letters focused on the importance of values, attitude, preparation, and perseverance. He believed the joy of living is in doing and, whenever possible, in being of service to others. Further themes in the letters included the will to win, integrity, selflessness, goal setting, motivation, determination, character, and faith. The letters contain his philosophy of life and system of values, which stood as the foundation for his remarkable success as a coach and helped him deal with his own personal challenges, not only in football but also later in life.

The times, obviously, have changed, but since the lessons contained in these letters remain pertinent, I asked myself: What principles concerning parenting, mentoring, leadership, excellence, and success had my dad shared with me that I could pass along to others? How could an understanding of what guided him in his philosophy of life help executives, managers, parents, teachers, coaches, and mentors today, just as his ideas helped to mold his players and his sons a half century ago? Whether in professional careers or personal lives, people today are tasked with making important leadership decisions that shape the lives of others.

In an earlier book, *Bud Wilkinson: An Intimate Portrait of an American Legend*, I explained what made my father "tick" and how he became a success in so many different fields of endeavor, from sports to politics to broadcasting to business. This book is different. His intimate and personal letters reveal a father's consistent love, compassion, and understanding. They demonstrate his efforts to build a son's confidence and to help that son find his own path for the future. They stress the importance of providing worthwhile service to others while being engaged and active on a day-to-day basis in ways that bring personal satisfaction, happiness, and fulfillment. Beyond correcting an occasional misspelled word or mistake, the letters are presented just as he wrote them.

This book is not meant to glamorize my father. On the contrary, it is a deeply revealing look at the personal side of a man who was very famous in his time. More important, it offers discernment of a leadership style that can be employed throughout a wide variety of life pursuits.

Communication today, thanks in large part to technology, is becoming more compressed, abbreviated, and impersonal. In the past, handwritten letters were an important way for people to stay connected to one another. That my dad, an exceptionally busy person, would take time to write to his sons on a frequent and consistent basis, sometimes during great challenges in his life, shows another key dimension of the man. Writing these letters took time, but he knew it was important for him to take the time. Through his letters he provided me with reassurance and clarity, something not always achieved in a phone call or even a face-to-face discussion.

I hope that his philosophy and lessons for life contained in these letters will help guide you to become a better parent, manager, teacher, employee, neighbor, student, friend, and person. I know they helped me.

Dear Jay,

Love Dad

PART I

Freshman Year

1960–1961

> Only in the agony of parting do we look into the depths of love.
>
> Mary Ann Evans, author of the classic *Silas Marner*, written under her pen name George Eliot

My father, Bud Wilkinson, was not your run-of-the-mill football coach. He cast a sizable shadow across the Oklahoma landscape and that of college football as a whole. His teams won in prodigious fashion and he led his teams in innovative ways.

As a tall, graceful, and handsome young man, he stepped off the train in Norman in 1946 and looked at his new surroundings with both uncertainty and confidence. After being honorably discharged as a naval officer in World War II, Dad came to the University of Oklahoma as an assistant coach to Jim Tatum. After one year, and at the age of just thirty-one, he became head coach of the Sooners.

Through his leadership and personality he quickly began to make significant and decisive changes in the program. He had a unique style and approach; a certain grace, spirit, and diplomacy that transformed not only an athletic program and a university but also an entire state. As his teams began winning with consistency, with the victories came a rebirth of the citizenry's enthusiasm, confidence, and pride. Rodgers and Hammerstein's groundbreaking musical *Oklahoma!* had begun promoting a positive and popularized image of the state only a few years earlier, and Oklahomans were quick to embrace the new self-esteem that both the musical and the football wins generated.

Growing up, my brother Pat and I were affectionately known as "Bud's boys," sons to Mary and Charles "Bud" Wilkinson. While it would be easy to say we were the typical middle-class and middle-American family down the street, the truth was that none of our friends had fathers who were nationally famous or were featured on the covers of prominent magazines of the day. My father was Dad to us, but he also carried the title Coach for his University of Oklahoma football players and was more universally known to sporting enthusiasts throughout Oklahoma and across the country simply as Bud.

As Bud's boys, we held ourselves to self-imposed higher standards than our peers, both at home and in the community. Fortunately, we were almost never an embarrassment to our parents. This is not to say that we did not have our fair share of fun. But in growing up with the legendary Bud Wilkinson as your father, you had a pretty good idea of what was expected.

By the time I was a senior in high school, Dad's teams had made a habit of winning. In fact, it was not until Halloween of my senior year in 1959 that he finally lost his first conference game. And yet, his Sooners still won their thirteenth consecutive conference championship that year. He definitely knew something about winning, both on the scoreboard and in his own personal affairs.

My father was extremely well organized. He famously taught that the will to prepare is more important than the will to win. Through a soft-spoken and professorial-yet-believable manner he instructed his players always to do their best; to conduct themselves as gentlemen; and to treat others with kindness, dignity, and respect. His leadership skills were constantly in evidence based on the actions he took and the examples he set. He made time for and truly cared about the people around him.

Oklahoma has a proud Native American heritage. The state name comes from the Choctaw words *okla,* meaning "people," and *humma*, meaning "red." The so-called Five Civilized Tribes settled there—or were forcibly relocated—before the territory became a state in 1907. There were members of as many as twenty-six other tribes also scattered throughout the state. Dad's players, with the enthusiastic support of Indian leaders in the state, dubbed him "The Great White Father," a term of reverence and respect for his wisdom, towering presence, and preternaturally silver hair.

Winning at OU did not happen by accident, nor was it the only thing that mattered. Dad constantly emphasized to his squad that the primary reason they were in school was to get an education. He treated players on the fourth and fifth teams the same way he treated players on the first team—with esteem and respect. My older brother and I knew the way he spoke to his players was the same way he communicated with us. It was not that Dad was rigid and demanding with his sons. On the contrary: it was that he treated his players like family.

At Norman High School, my teams finished as state runners-up in football and state champions in basketball. My desire was to continue pursuit of that kind of success, at least in football, on the college level. The easy, natural, and obvious choice would have been for me to become a Sooner. I was the number one football recruit in the state of Oklahoma. There was a good chance that I would be in line to earn the starting quarterback position at OU since I was familiar and comfortable with Dad's offensive scheme.

Because of his iconic status as a coach, my father felt the pressures on his sons would be enormous if we attended the University of Oklahoma. Pat left home for college first, two years ahead of me. Injuries curtailed his athletic pursuits, and so he chose to head west to Palo Alto, California, and Stanford University, where his academic studies ultimately led him to a successful medical career as an acclaimed ophthalmologist. My circumstances were different. Although Dad went on record with the family saying he believed I would be wise to go off to college, he ultimately left that decision in my hands.

With an intimate knowledge of the OU program, my recruiting trips took me to Stanford, UCLA, Ole Miss, Illinois, and West Point, all top-caliber football schools at the time. Shortly before a visit to the U.S. Military Academy, I got a phone call from Duke University's assistant athletic director, Carl James, making an eleventh-hour recruiting pitch. When I told him about my intent to visit West Point, he suggested I make a stop in Durham on the way. Carl was persuasive and I agreed to visit his school.

Something magical happened on my stopover at Duke. The campus was beautiful. There, they acknowledged me both as a prospective athlete *and* as a student. Duke was the only college to recruit me academically. James arranged for me to spend a significant amount of time with the chair of the school's history department and the dean of men, each of whom made a strong and positive impression.

The Duke football program of my day was highly regarded, playing a top-flight schedule each year. In the 1958 Orange Bowl I had watched the Atlantic Coast Conference champion Blue Devils battle the Sooners. Oklahoma won 48–21, but the game was much closer than the final score. Although I traveled to North Carolina regarding Duke as nothing more than an afterthought, I left thinking that I would probably become a Blue Devil.

Still, the final decision was painful and difficult. In my heart, I had a great love for the University of Oklahoma. For more than a dozen years I had dreamed of one day playing for my father. Yet in the end, I sided with him; going away to school was probably the right decision. Just as he was concerned about my well-being if I became a Sooner, I also was worried that I could become a distraction for him, particularly if he was ever accused of giving me preferential treatment. When Dad came into my bedroom shortly after my visit to Duke, I burst into tears and told him how much I wanted to play for him, but that I had reached my conclusion and decided it would be best for me—and for him—if I went away to school. I remember his support, kindness, and comforting words as his strong hands rubbed my back. A few days later a headline in the *Daily Oklahoman's* sports section proclaimed: "Jay Wilkinson to go to Duke."

On my way to begin classes and freshman football at Duke, I truly felt alone for the first time in my young life. I knew that my feelings of separation were normal and similar to those of other teenagers leaving home to start a new job, join the military, or simply find themselves. What was not normal was leaving a football tradition that had been part of my emotional makeup since my family's arrival in Norman when I was four. Thirteen years later, Dad's teams had achieved an incredible record of 121–13–3; a winning rate of almost 93 percent!

I was at the beginning of a journey that would take me from everyone and everything I knew in Norman, Oklahoma, to the great unknown of my freshman year at Duke University in Durham, North Carolina. Bud's boys were soon to be three thousand miles apart.

Dad and I were very close before I left home for Duke, but my life-defining "coming-of-age" chats would take place, in large part, over the next six years in the series of handwritten letters he sent to me at school. During and after those years, it slowly occurred to me that my father's success was not defined by his achievements on the field. It was shaped by his wisdom, his understanding, his compassion, and his love.

The letters that follow take you through a crucial time of my life, during which my father's consistent emotional support and personal leadership made a true difference in helping me deal with change and cope with failure. The substance of these letters also became a framework for the life I would lead as an adult, with his words indelibly etched in my mind and his abiding love always carried in my heart.

His first letter responded to my concern after arriving at Duke and being a typically lonesome and homesick young man who had a hard time transitioning to a new coaching philosophy and way of doing things.

Entering the Unknown

September, 1960

Dear Jay,

It was good to talk to you—I know things will get better because you are the kind of person who can adjust and find the good in all situations.

When I read your letter, I recalled vividly many similar times in my life. When I left home to go to Shattuck, I was truly blue. Yet I know now how fine a thing it was for me and my future. The training I received has made my life good. When I left you, Pat, and Mother to go to sea during the war, I was really shaken. I loved you and wanted to watch you and help you as you grew up—and I was leaving not knowing if I'd ever get back again. But once more, the experience and training I received more than compensated for the heartaches. Then too, I had the personal satisfaction of knowing I had done my duty.

One of the first things an education brings to people is the realization that the world is a big place—full of many different ideas and ways of doing things. You have watched our team practice and quite naturally are attuned to our ways of doing things. Bill Murray has been a fine coach for many years. Instead of wondering why they do things differently, you should be studying what they do so you will understand that their approach will get the job done more effectively—maybe more easily than we can.

When any person leaves a pleasant situation to enter the "unknown," there is always the realization of how nice, good and comfortable things were before. Yet only by facing the future and accepting new and progressively more difficult challenges are we able to grow, develop, and avoid stagnation. You have more total, all-around ability in all fields than anyone I have ever known. You will certainly be a great man and make a great contribution to the world.

But to do this you must take on new and progressively more difficult challenges. You will grow and develop in direct relationship to the way you meet and overcome what at first seem to be hard assignments. You will learn to love Duke—to take great pride in the school and their football team. You're that kind of person. By developing as a student and an athlete, you will prepare yourself to do bigger and better things when you graduate.

Always remember that I believe in you no matter what. You must do what seems right to you. Don't ever be swayed by what "other people will think." My grandmother, a great lady—one of the finest I've ever known—always told me when I was a young boy growing up to "dare to be a Daniel; dare to stand alone." It is the best advice one can have for happy, successful living. After analyzing and evaluating the circumstances—always do what seems best to you in the light of your own good judgment. Only in this way can you find peace of mind because you cannot be happy doing "what other people think you should do." You must do what you think you should do.

I didn't quite finish this letter yesterday before practice so am doing so this morning, Saturday. Norman tied Capitol Hill last night 26–26. They miss their "Big Tiger" on defense—as well as offense.

I love you, Jay, more than anything in life. Don't worry about things—live each day by doing your best. Will look forward to talking to you tomorrow.

Love always,
Dad

When I arrived for my freshman year at Duke, I was the proverbial stranger in a strange land. The University of Oklahoma was a state-supported school located less than two miles from my home; Duke was a private institution founded in 1832 and nestled in the Piedmont region of North Carolina, about three hours west of the Atlantic Ocean.

The sons and daughters of some of the nation's leading families attended Duke. Beginning with my senior year, 1963, the school opened its doors to racial integration. Academically, Duke is ranked today among the nation's top institutions of higher learning. Such was the case in my day as well. A degree from Duke was and is on par with those from any of the finest schools along the East Coast.

Athletically, the Duke of my day was known for the success of both its football and basketball programs. Football coach Bill Murray won seven conference titles in the 1950s and early 1960s, including Orange Bowl and Cotton Bowl victories, and was respected as one of the finest coaches in the country. Basketball coach Vic Bubas, who arrived at Duke one year before me, quickly built the basketball program into a powerhouse, achieving an Atlantic Coast Conference tournament record of 22–6 and a Cameron Indoor Stadium record of 87–13 during the next ten years. The basketball team, now legendary under the direction of Coach Mike Krzyzewski, would later claim four national titles.

Arriving at Duke's Wallace Wade Stadium, I was accustomed to Dad's offensive and defensive philosophies at Oklahoma, the rhythms of his practices, and even the nature of the equipment his players used. For the first couple weeks, as I made my way from the locker room to the Duke practice field everything around me seemed all wrong. It was like turning one's nose up at a delicious homemade cobbler simply because it was not like the ones Mom used to bake.

Dad's first letter to me at school was as welcome a sight as one of Mom's homemade desserts would have been. In the dorm room I shared with fellow freshman football player Kenny Stewart, a mountain of a young man from West Virginia, I eagerly opened the envelope and unfolded the letter, written on Dad's University of Oklahoma head coach stationery.

My father's character had been shaped in many ways: by family, by his time spent away from home at boarding school, by his multifaceted college experience, and by his service to country as a naval officer in World War II. His demand for excellence was sizable, both from himself and from those for whom he bore responsibility, but he never led with a whip. Encouragement and positive reinforcement defined his leadership style, and I would come to understand better, appreciate, and embrace that philosophy during my time at Duke.

In his words I held before me, Dad's reassurance was soothing. His endorsement of Duke football coach Bill Murray was important. His faith in me was profound. I could also identify with the feelings of sadness he shared with me. It had been hard on him to leave home as a boy to attend prep school at Shattuck in Faribault, Minnesota, but it had helped to prepare him for what was to come. I knew full well about his experiences serving on the *USS Enterprise* in the Iwo Jima and Okinawa campaigns of World War II. He had come close to dying in a kamikaze attack on his aircraft carrier, but he had survived, unlike many with whom he served. He came through those experiences tougher and wiser, and he wanted the same kind of growth for me.

Away from home myself, I began to gain new perspective, realizing that the world was a much bigger place than I had ever imagined. I was coming to grips with the fact that life was filled with complexities, ambiguities, and at times, sadness. How people adjust and find the good in all things was an important quality and a key ingredient in maintaining happiness. When times are tough, I knew, there was a natural tendency to withdraw, surrender, and feel sorry for oneself. Dad's focus remained upbeat and optimistic. His guidance and support helped me understand that only by accepting new and progressively more challenging circumstances are people able to develop and grow as individuals.

I began to look differently at my personal situation. My pride in and love for my new school validated both my father's counsel and my decision to find my own way in life. I liked and respected my classmates, teammates, coaches, and professors. Most important, leaving home enabled me to acquaint myself with the fact that taking on new responsibilities was the natural order of life.

Dad's reminder, "Always remember, I believe in you no matter what," was a pivotal one. Encouragement and positive reinforcement are central elements in motivating others. His advocacy instilled in me a greater self-confidence, just as his teams' successes had enabled the people of Oklahoma to see themselves in a different light.

Above all things, Dad encouraged me always to do what seemed right. Only by doing so, he said, could a person possess true peace of mind. In rereading the letter decades later, it was obvious to me that my father was preparing me for success, not only in my coming years as a football player but also in the larger scheme of my future.

Academically, my first semester at Duke unfolded better than I had reason to expect. Duke's assistant athletic director, Carl James, the man largely responsible for my decision to attend the school, helped enroll me in classes with some of the university's most respected professors in political science, English, history, religion, and French. Athletes at Duke were expected then, as they are today, to carry a full course load and to meet the same academic curriculum requirements as all other students.

Among incoming fellow students I came to know and like were Charlie Rose, today a respected and award-winning broadcast journalist; Pete Nicholas, co-founder and chairman of the medical device firm Boston Scientific; and Jeff Mullins, one in a long line of basketball greats to have graced the hallowed court of Cameron Indoor Stadium and one of the fifty greatest basketball players in Atlantic Coast Conference history.

Athletically, my adjustments on the football field were made easier by the fact that freshmen were ineligible to play varsity athletics. My fellow freshmen and I were sequestered from many activities relating to the varsity squad. First-year players practiced as a unit and played a complement of five games against freshmen teams from other universities in the area. I took the majority of the freshman snaps as quarterback and led the team to a respectable record of 4–1.

I had established myself among my football teammates and coaches as a promising talent and potential leader. I acquitted myself well in the classroom, ultimately finishing the first semester among the top 10 percent of my class. I felt satisfied and happy with my surroundings, but as the autumn progressed, I again found myself spending time second-guessing my decision to leave home.

In Norman, Dad's Oklahoma Sooners had entered uncharted territory. OU went 3–6–1 during the 1960 campaign. They lost to Iowa State for the first time in twenty-eight years. They were shut out by Colorado, marking the first time since 1942 that OU had failed to score in a conference game. It was an enormous contrast to what Dad had experienced in the preceding thirteen years as head coach.

And as the season progressed, I felt as if this was partly my fault. With every Sooner setback that season, I felt a greater sense of guilt and a greater obligation to be at my dad's side, not only as his son but as his recruit. My leaving home made all the sense in the world until Dad's losses began to mount. He needed a good option quarterback, and I felt that I was that player. It made no difference that as a freshman I would have been ineligible to play for him in 1960. I thought my presence would somehow have made a difference.

Duke, meanwhile, was enjoying a banner season, one that culminated with the Atlantic Coast Conference championship and a triumph over Arkansas in the Cotton Bowl on a last minute touchdown pass to Duke All American Tee Moorman. One of the biggest wins of the year was a 19–10 victory over a Navy team featuring that year's eventual Heisman Trophy winner, Joe Bellino.

After that game, I wove my way through the throng of Duke students and fans who had rushed the field in celebration. I found the familiar face I had been looking for. J. D. Roberts was an All American guard and Outland Trophy winner for Dad in 1953 and had later been an assistant coach for him at OU. By 1960 he was an assistant at Navy. I needed to talk to him.

When Roberts saw me approaching, a big smile crossed his face, but the smile quickly vanished as he saw my somber countenance. He greeted me with a reminder that it was a good day to be a Blue Devil. "J.D., I'm concerned about Dad and I think maybe I should transfer back to OU," I blurted out. "He needs me and I should be there for him."

Amidst the pandemonium around us, Roberts placed his arm around my shoulders. His advice was simple and straightforward: "Jay, you made the right decision in coming to Duke. Yes, your dad's team is struggling this year, and, yes, you're an outstanding player. But in the four years I played for Coach Wilkinson, he never once made football just about winning. Your dad's going to be fine, and you're going to have a great career as a Blue Devil."

Roberts was right. Dad was okay. He was exactly the same man in losing that he had been in winning all those years. After the season ended, Pat and I joined Mom and Dad at home for an enjoyable Christmas break. In spite of the season's disappointments, Dad was upbeat, and our family celebrated the holidays with the same gusto, festive singing, and joyful spirit as when OU had been winning. And Mom's homemade cherry cobbler tasted extra good.

Soon Mom and Dad would be on a well-deserved relaxing trip away from the pressures of football.

⋘⋙

A Winning Habit

January 18, 1961—Wednesday

Dear Jay,

Our trip has been most restful and peaceful. I've had more sleep and rest than I can recall in many years. I haven't been on a scale, but I'm afraid I've gained quite a bit of weight. Except for that everything has been good.

I met Mother in New Orleans last Tuesday, the ship was supposed to sail Wednesday, but as freighters do—there was a day's delay and we didn't get off until Thursday night. New Orleans is famous for their many fine restaurants and we took advantage of the extra day to eat at all of the fine places. Both Mother and I like seafood. We had oysters and shrimp cooked in rich, but delicately flavored sauces— trout, crab meat, etc. I doubt if you would have ordered what we did—except at breakfast when we had Eggs Benedict each morning. They weren't quite as good as those we had at the Plaza Hotel in New York City last summer.

There were 10 other passengers on the ship—a retired Army Colonel and wife, Nancy Kelly, who I guess is a former movie star and her husband—a couple from Michigan—and one from Chicago together with a young man from Chicago named Morton and his mother. Morton is 22. He is on the police force in Chicago and he is an expert on everything. He did add a great deal of life to the group in spite of confusing us with his hard-headed opinions and stories of his varied talents.

We didn't do anything except take our baths, eat, sleep, and read. The weather after the first day was warm and wonderful. Mom wasn't seasick, and we thoroughly enjoyed ourselves. Breakfast was served at 7:30, lunch at 11:30, and dinner at 5. I was in bed each night by 8.

The ship docked in San Juan at 7 A.M. Thursday. We drove out here to the hotel which took about an hour. It is a spectacularly beautiful place. It was an old plantation. Laurance Rockefeller bought it five years ago and built it into a resort. The hotel fronts on the sea with a much better beach than Waikiki. There is a large pool and a difficult but truly lovely golf course. Actually, I don't think the course would be too tough if I had had a chance to play more. I shot 88 yesterday and 84 today—but I did hit the ball quite well. There had been quite a bit of rain prior to our arrival and the course was almost too wet to let it be fun to play yesterday. Today, it had dried quite a bit, but we were still walking in water part of the time.

We leave tomorrow morning and drive across the island to a town called Ponce. The ship is supposed to sail from there tomorrow afternoon. We will land in Mobile on Monday and should get home Tuesday or Wednesday.

I brought your book, *Preface to Philosophy,* with me and am enjoying reading it. One paragraph from William James' essay on habits should be of value to you. In case you haven't read it, I'll quote it for you.

"Let no youth have an anxiety about the upshot of his education, whatever the line of it may be. If he keeps faithfully busy each hour of the working day, he may safely leave the final result to itself. He can with perfect certainty plan on waking up some fine morning to find himself one of the competent ones of his generation, in whatever pursuit he may have singled out. Silently between all the details of his business the *power* of *judging* in all that class of matter will have built itself up within him as a possession that will never pass away. Young people should know this truth in advance. The ignorance of it has probably engendered more discouragement and faint heartedness in youths embarking on arduous careers than all other causes put together."

I know you're busy studying for exams. Will be pulling for you. If you do your best—and I know you will—your work will be excellent.

Mother and I are still talking about how much fun we had at Christmas when you and Pat were home. We're looking forward to Easter. She joins me in sending our love to our wonderful son.

> Love always,
> Dad

The life of a head football coach is uniquely strenuous and demanding. Aside from the pressure of winning, a coach has many different tasks fully occupying his time during the season, from preparing game plans and organizing and managing players and assistant coaches to the actual game day work on the sideline and then dealing with media, alumni, and school administrators after the game. For Dad, additional responsibilities usually included a post-season game, recruiting, conducting Coach-of-the-Year clinics, television shows, speaking engagements, and other appearances. He used to say that a coach had one of the toughest jobs in the country because he had to please so many different people: players, parents, the university president and board of regents, faculty, and fans.

One upside to coaching, as my parents gratefully learned, was the opportunity to unwind and relax in the off-season. On the trip to San Juan and Dorado Beach, Puerto Rico, Dad could put behind him the disappointment of his first losing season—as either a coach or a player—and treat Mom to a wonderful cruise. The fact that he slept soundly and enjoyed the company of strangers, even a young know-it-all cop from the Windy City of Chicago, spoke volumes about his character. It never really wavered through victory or defeat.

Whether he intended this or not, there was deep meaning in almost everything he wrote to me during my college years. Putting aside football and his need to right the Sooners' own ship, he brought to life the words of the American psychologist and philosopher William James, setting for me a real-world example that if one was doing one's level best, one could "safely leave the final result to itself."

Today I understand the value of James's philosophy better. It is clear and precise and applies to every discipline and endeavor, whether academic, athletic, business, military, medical, governmental, educational, spiritual, or personal. And it applies during both good times and bad.

⋖⋛⋗

Decisions

2/17/1961—Thursday

Dear Jay,

I was sorry I missed your call last night. I had to be in Muskogee for the Annual QB Club Banquet. I'm on my way now to Grand Rapids, Michigan for our second Coaching School.

Congratulations on pledging Phi Delt. It is a fine fraternity nationally—and from all I've heard—it is without doubt the best at Duke.

I can imagine the pressures you were subjected to, but I hope they weren't too tough. While I know it wasn't always pleasant, such things are fine and profitable experiences.

Does Spring Practice begin on Tuesday? Mother couldn't recall exactly what you had said. Don't worry about not being in good enough shape—what position you'll play—or whether you'll make the team. Simply do your dead-level best every single day at practice—make your continued best effort—be tough—and everything will work out perfectly. I'll be anxious to hear about it.

I have a problem which is surprising and difficult. Yesterday, a man named Ted Reardon called me from the White House and asked me, on behalf of the President, to become the Executive Director for Youth Fitness. This would be a Presidential appointment. I would be working under Secretary Ribicoff, who is the Cabinet Officer of Health, Recreation and Welfare.

There is no doubt that it is a fine opportunity to make a contribution for a cause in which I believe, but if I accept I will probably have to give up my job at Oklahoma, move to Washington, make only 1/3 as much money while residing in a far more expensive place, and then be out of a job in four or eight years when we have a new President.

It is an honor to be even considered for such a position. I'm going to Washington after the Clinics to talk with Mr. Reardon about it. I'll call you when I know a little more as I would like to know what you think before I accept or refuse. In the meantime, please don't tell anybody.

Everything else seems to be coming along quite well. Mom's back is OK—our recruiting is going quite well—we had fairly good scholastic grades by our players last semester. I'm anxious to see our new men in Spring Practice.

We received your grades from Duke today. I was truly proud—and you should be too. Keep up the good work.

We'll talk to you soon.

Love always,
Dad

My father always put family over football. It was no surprise that he got around to his own big news only after apologizing for missing my call, congratulating me on the soon-to-be-improved circumstances of my social life, and inquiring about my upcoming "work" schedule. A new opportunity from the President of the United States does not come along every week. Even more notable than his manner of relating the news was his interest in getting my reaction to it.

Given Dad's success as a coach and his wide range of interests off the field, it was natural enough that unique and enticing opportunities would come his way. They had for years; he bypassed most to focus on building and sustaining his football program. A job offer from the president, however, was a different matter. But Dad was not the only one faced with a pressing decision.

Part of the total college experience at Duke for a large percentage of students is membership in a social sisterhood or brotherhood. "Rush," the process of recruiting prospective members into these fraternal organizations, took place in my years at school between the end of first-semester exams and the beginning of the spring session. The means of gaining entry into one of these fraternal organizations was similar to what I had experienced going through the recruiting process: it was a bit of a popularity contest, and the path chosen by others whom I knew and respected mattered greatly to me.

Phi Delta Theta and Kappa Alpha were the fraternities to which 90 percent of the Duke football players belonged. While there were many other excellent fraternities on campus, my choice boiled down to the fact that three of my junior teammates who had made a strong and favorable impression on me during my first semester were Phi Delts.

Gary Wilson was a talented halfback. Everything about him was first class, and I was not alone in my admiration for the example he set. Such was likewise true of hardworking fullback and linebacker Roy Bostock, a member of the Duke baseball team, who besides being a Phi Delt was honored as a Phi Beta Kappa for academic excellence. I also had the privilege of playing with guard Rex Adams during my sophomore season at Duke. Adams led our team and fraternity in academic achievement too; he graduated *magna cum laude* before earning postgraduate placement at Oxford University as a Rhodes scholar.

Finer role models one could not hope to find. In later years Adams was an executive with Mobil before becoming dean of the Duke Fuqua School of Business. At the time of writing he chaired the board of Invesco, a multi-billion-dollar investment management company, and was former chairman of the board for the Public Broadcasting Service. Wilson, after successful executive careers with the Marriott and Disney corporations, became chairman of Northwest Airlines and served as a trustee emeritus at Duke University and a member of the board of trustees of the NCAA's Leadership Advisory Board. Bostock became chairman of Yahoo! Inc. The Bostock Library on the Duke campus is named for him and his wife, Merilee.

One of the things in life that I may have learned outside my father's wisdom and counsel is that people are known by the company they keep. John Kennedy made an offer to my father because he saw in him a potential "reflected glow" that would translate favorably to the objectives and high-minded ideals of the new presidential administration.

At that same time, my choices as a college freshman exposed me to exceptional people who would go on to become extraordinary leaders—not just from Phi Delta Theta or Kappa Alpha but also from within many other on-campus organizations. And while Dad was correct in observing that the rush hoopla was indeed stressful, his optimistic attitude that such events could be "fine and profitable experiences" was once again on the mark. He always found the good in any situation.

⬧⬦⬧

Seventh Team

2/25/1961—Saturday P.M.

Dear Jay,

We've just completed our Dallas clinic and I've a few minutes before leaving for the airport and home. Right now, you're probably in the midst of scrimmage. I hope you're doing well.

I was very concerned to hear about how much weight you had lost. I hope you can regain some of it while practice is going on. Don't be concerned about starting off on the 7th team—or on what team you play. Simply, do what we talked about at Christmas—your best every day at whatever you are doing—be a leader and be tough. If you approach the game in this manner, you can't miss.

I'm sort of concerned about your getting behind in your studies. I hope you don't because it's hard to catch up. It is much easier to do your work every day—as you did the first semester.

Since returning from Washington, I've drawn up a proposed plan for Youth fitness and have forwarded it to the White House. If Reardon, the President's Aide, doesn't like it, I'll have no further problem. If he does, I may have to go to Washington part-time to get the program under way. I don't believe, after thinking the matter through, that I could do any more good full-time than part-time—and since Dr. Cross will give me time off—the most difficult part of the problem appears to be solved. I'll let you know what Washington decides, as soon as I hear anything.

We think of you often and are looking forward to Easter.

> All my love, always
> Dad

PS: You're the finest son a Father ever had—I'm so proud of you.

Having experienced great success in high school and on the Duke freshman squad, I was disappointed to find myself on the seventh team depth chart at the beginning of spring practice. But I knew that it was not as unusual as it might have seemed. As was commonplace at the time, Coach Murray employed a "redshirt" system, which meant the majority of players were withheld from competition during their sophomore year at school without losing that year's eligibility. This gave them an extra year to mature and develop physically and to learn the system better before actual varsity competition. It also meant that there would be more quality depth on the team, since it would include five classes instead of four.

Over the holidays Dad had pointed out that Duke had a number of excellent players at the quarterback position and that I would need to be patient to earn playing time. As it turned out, our two top quarterbacks, Walt Rappold and Gil Garner, would lead the Atlantic Coast Conference in passing percentage during the 1961 season. The ACC included several other standout quarterbacks that year, among them Roman Gabriel at North Carolina State,

Norm Snead at Wake Forest, and Dick Shiner at Maryland, all of whom were great college players and would later enjoy successful NFL careers.

Dad knew my first spring with the Duke varsity was important, and his advice continued to be consistent: be a leader, be tough, and be the best you can be every day at whatever you do. I knew those words were the same ones he used to motivate his Oklahoma players, and they provided me with the inspiration to succeed. The twenty spring practices were physically demanding, but through the experience I learned even more about Coach Murray's approach to the game.

Academics at Duke were challenging, and although I had an excellent first semester in class, Dad was aware that I was beginning to struggle. Not only did he stress the importance of keeping up with my studies, but he also encouraged me to seek balance among the many demands on my time. Thus began a dialogue about my classroom performance that would continue throughout my time at Duke.

Thirst for Knowledge

February 28, 1961

Dear Jay,

We enjoyed your fine letter. I believe your suggestion of reading each day and then having a family discussion is excellent. The thirst for knowledge which you now have will probably never be quenched. I am appalled at my lack of wisdom in innumerable areas. I try to read something worthwhile each day—but I fall further behind and understand less as I read more. It will be an intellectually stimulating, growing experience to follow your suggestion. I hope we do it. We can if we budget our time properly.

Don't be concerned about your football. The reason you practice is to improve—to learn to execute better. If you keep trying every day, you'll get better. It's a gradual development—hard to recognize from day to day—but easy to see from week to week.

When you come up on defense—don't even think about playing off the blockers. Come up so fast—with so much determination to get the ball carrier—that your speed and aggressiveness will carry you through or past the blockers. Try this—and see how it works.

Had another call this morning from the White House. They had read and liked my plan. They want me to take a year's leave of absence—but I don't see how I can. I think I could do the job part-time—but I doubt if this will be acceptable to them. I'm going to talk to Dr. Cross this afternoon and will talk to Washington tomorrow or Thursday. I'll call if and when anything serious develops.

Hope your studies are coming along well. We miss you—love you—and are looking forward to Easter.

Love always,
Dad

When guests were invited to our home as Pat and I grew up, there was never a "kids' table." Dinner conversations evolved around things of substance other than football and included lively discussions on such matters as international, political, religious, and human-interest issues. We learned to be on our toes and prepared to debate. Small wonder that my brother was co-valedictorian of his high school graduating class and was thriving in the rigorous academic environment at Stanford University. In our coast-to-coast telephone calls, Pat and I would compare notes concerning campus life. I always made sure he realized that being a student at Duke was no walk in the park when it came to expectations in the classroom.

During the spring semester of my freshman year, when I took the time to focus on my studies, I found almost all my courses stimulating and of interest. Although I was not as advanced intellectually as either my father or brother, with my growing assimilation of new knowledge and understanding, I was eager to participate, even long distance, in the kinds of discussions my father so enjoyed.

I knew that his communication skills were an essential part of his leadership capabilities. In many ways this was what set him apart from so many of his peers. He understood that to inspire a young athlete to greatness, one had to motivate body, mind, and spirit.

As a youngster, Dad inherited a love for literature from his father, C.P. Throughout his life he returned repeatedly to books his father had introduced to him in childhood, such nonchildish works as *The World's Famous Orations* edited by William Jennings Bryan and Christopher Marlowe's *Masterpieces of the English Drama*. Books like these, even in his youth, piqued his interest in communication and in English.

With that solid foundation, Dad excelled academically during his prep school days at Shattuck Military Academy, where he won the Harvard Cup for athletic and scholastic achievement. While at the University of Minnesota he won the Big Ten Medal, the school's highest honor for combined academic and athletic excellence. Later, while a graduate assistant coach at the University of Syracuse, he received his master's degree in English education. After his formal education Dad continued his interest in a wide variety of intellectual disciplines for the remainder of his life. In the mid-1950s he purchased *Great Books of the Western World* published by Encyclopædia Britannica. This library of fifty-four classics featured a diverse set of works from Homer, Plato, and Aristotle to Tolstoy, Dostoevsky, James, and Freud.

Dad knew that the road to wisdom and enlightenment came through a deep understanding of the context of great works of literature. For many years he took time to study the *Great Books* in order to enhance his mental acuity. Through these efforts he developed a greater understanding of the fact that many big questions do not have easy answers. He also possessed a deep humility as to his own lack of wisdom in so many areas. But he tried. I remember him tirelessly reading from the *Great Books* and keeping notes on a variety of subjects. His emphasis on learning, both inside and outside the classroom, prompted Pat and me to take learning seriously in college and afterward.

Dad continued to keep me in the loop concerning his impending White House appointment. I was confident the issue could be resolved to everyone's satisfaction because he was operating from a position of strength. President Kennedy wanted him for the post, and OU president Dr. George L. Cross certainly did not want to lose him as the head football coach. A compromise seemed the logical conclusion.

⋘⋙

Failure as a Possibility

3/16/1961—In flight—Sunday night

Dear Jay,

After our Conference Meeting and the Coaching Clinic in Kansas City, I came on to Washington to talk with Ted Reardon, the President's Executive Assistant and a Mr. Nestingen, the Under Secretary of Health, Education and Welfare concerning the Fitness

Program. I met with them this afternoon for about three hours.

I told them I couldn't, for many reasons, take the job full time—but that I would be glad to work as a consultant in setting up the program. I guess I told you that I had sent them a proposal as to how to attack the problem. They apparently like it—and it looks as though they'll take me up on the offer. I will be serving without pay—and will probably be gone from home a lot—especially during the summer—but if they want me—I guess I should give it a try. After the organization is set up—I don't believe it will take too much time to keep it operating.

I'm supposed to write a brief summary of my proposal which they will then send to the President's Council—which is made up of 6 Cabinet members. If these men concur with the program—and will support it—I'm going to appear before them to briefly answer questions concerning it at which time it will be announced that I'm the Advisor to the Council.

Actually, I'm torn about it. If they don't like my plan, I'm free to do my own job. If they do like it, I'm trapped for a lot of extra work— at which I may fail. We'll just have to wait and see how it comes out. I'll let you know, if and when I hear anything.

How is spring practice? I've been thinking about you, and wondering how you were getting along. I'll call—maybe before you get this letter—as I want to hear all about it. I'm sure you'll do well in FB. I just hope you won't let your studies get too far ahead of you.

Mom is in Grinnell, but will be home Tuesday. Write when you can. Will talk with you soon.

> All my love always,
> Dad

In a sense, Dad was looking to take a "second job" as he continued to explore becoming the head of the President's Council on

Physical Fitness. On the one hand, his OU team had never been in greater need of his attention, having concluded the 1960 season with his first losing season ever. Yet he was intrigued by the possibility of a presidential appointment and saw great potential in the program he was considering. Unwilling to leave his players after a poor season, he hoped he could manage both his on- and off-field responsibilities. Ever the realist, Dad knew there existed the chance of failure—at both pursuits.

He understood that the difference between victory and defeat can be a very narrow margin. Beginning in 1948 and extending through the 1958 season, Dad's teams lost only eight times, and none of those defeats was by more than a touchdown. If not for a seven-point setback in 1957 and a one-point loss in 1958, Oklahoma's record win streak would have been sixty-two consecutive games, not forty-seven straight. He knew the difference between success and failure in pursuits away from the athletic field could also be razor thin. While confident of the plan he was putting into place, he knew he would be representing the White House from a position of disadvantage.

When Dad took over the reins as head coach at OU he inherited a full squad of players, facilities, a budget, and supporters. In launching the President's Council on Fitness, virtually nothing was in place. The council had no statutory authority over school boards, teachers, or parents. Its success depended entirely on his ability to provide leadership in defining the critical importance of the organization's mission and in motivating many diverse interest groups to support the program passionately. Just as he did as a football coach, he did all in his power to assure that the program would have every opportunity to succeed.

Dad invited me to attend the congressional committee hearings in Washington, D.C., to approve the council's budget. All the early dialogue between Dad and the committee members was about football! Congressmen were proud of the established football traditions in their home districts, and these proved to be of enormous importance and interest. It was amusing to me that testimony on the council's budget did not begin in earnest until all accolades and metaphors had been exhausted, which took considerable time. Over the course of the hearings the program was ultimately given the green light.

Today many believe that no subsequent effort or program did as much as that of the Kennedy Administration to make the public aware of the need to address and improve physical fitness among both children and adults. Dad's honest and realistic assessment of the issue, and his skills at implementing the program, showed me that the factors making him successful as a coach were the same ingredients leading to his success off the field.

⋖⊱⋯⊰⋗

Red Tape

5/5/1961—Thursday

Dear Jay,

We had your good letter today. I was pleased you enjoyed Joe College weekend so much. College should be fun as well as work—as should life.

Our team is pretty well set for the Alumni Game. We have more alumni back than ever before. I guess they all want to be on T.V.! They do have quite a line-up. Their defensive backfield is Harris, Baker, Boyd and Thomas—not a bad group. On offense they have those men plus McDonald—Pricer—Gautt, etc. Tubbs, Harrison, Ed Gray, Ross Coyle, etc. are here too. I'm sure we'll cut them to ribbons!

I flew to Washington last Saturday and was there until Monday night. Things are beginning to shape up, but the Government red tape is quite complicated. There are man-made rules and regulations. All of them tell you what you can't do. It delays things terribly—but I'm sure once we get organized everything will be fine.

I hope you will be able to stop by Washington on your way home. While there, I rented a little house for the summer. We will move in when we arrive on the 15th so we'll have an extra bedroom. I'd like you to meet some of the people in Government.

Mom and I will try to come to Durham after we get to Washington. We'll call to make arrangements.

Hope your studies are coming well. Bob Lee told me you'd written about a job, it looks good now.

Love always,
Dad

Dad's letters of encouragement to me throughout my life got me writing letters as well. On frequent occasions in college I took time to write to my parents. The early 1960s featured no such things as e-mail, computers, cell phones, or even color TV. Students did not have phones in their dorm rooms, and the act of placing a long-distance phone call was both cumbersome and expensive. America was a long way from becoming a "fast-food nation" of intensifying demands for instant access, wealth, and gratification.

People had more patience then. And although the notion of red tape slowing down the wheels of progress was irksome to a man like my father, he knew patience could be a strong virtue in leadership. He was accustomed to guidelines and restrictions, administering his football program under the dictates of multiple governing bodies. Individuals might not agree with every circumstance and condition of their employment or labor, but an acceptance of these requirements with equanimity was critical to success.

One of OU's greatest football traditions in Dad's era was the annual varsity-alumni football game that brought an end to the program's rite of spring drills. Just as the name suggests, the game pitted the Sooners' current varsity squad against a team of alumni, many of whom were by then playing professional football, either in the National Football League or in Canada. Football fans of the time readily recognized the names in my father's letter, former Sooner greats Jerry Tubbs, Tommy McDonald, Clendon Thomas, Bob Harrison, and Prentice Gautt, to name just a few.

Today the NFL prohibits its players from participating in such games due to the possibility of injury. But in the 1950s and 1960s varsity-alumni games were almost as important to football fans as a school's regular-season schedule. The annual game in Norman enabled OU partisans not only to measure the progress made by the Sooner varsity squad during spring workouts but also to thrill at the return of past greats, the alumni players who had earlier brought Sooner fans so much enjoyment and pride.

My father felt there was another important benefit to the contest. The game helped foster a connection between past and present. In a real sense the program's tradition of excellence was forged, and a symbolic torch was passed, during the skirmishes that took place in these exhibition games pitting seasoned professionals against young men striving to live up to the legacy their predecessors had helped to create. Dad also knew, as did the varsity veterans of the spring showdown, that the talent differential between the two sides was never as great as might be imagined, due in part to the conditioning of the two teams. He felt this factor bolstered his team's confidence and assurance heading into the summer and the new season in the fall.

Half a continent away, Joe College Weekend at Duke was also a special time of year, a spring weekend devoted to matters less serious than football: music, laughter, games, and parties. During my undergraduate years the event attracted entertainers on par with and including Bob Hope. The value of events like this was not lost on my father. While he was an ardent proponent of the serious side of life—things like self-discipline, preparation, commitment, sacrifice, and hard work—he also constantly stressed that work and life should be fun too, which was one of the reasons he was so much fun to be with. He believed in the old adage about all work and no play leading to an unsatisfying existence. Dad demanded much from those with whom he worked in all endeavors, but he strongly encouraged his players, associates, and peers to enjoy the rewards of their labors fully and to embrace happiness and contentment as much as grit and toil.

⋖≫⋙⋗

Looking Forward to the Summer

May 1961

Dear Jay:

We enjoyed your letter. I know you're bearing down for exams and think it will be difficult to find time to write from now on.

Mom and I aren't going to Wichita until the morning of May 31. We'll make the flight on the 29th—Call us collect from Dallas to tell us which one you'll be on.

I'm on my way to NY to talk tomorrow to the Board of the Advertising Council regarding the Fitness Program. They are our biggest asset so I hope I'm able to do a reasonably effective job. I leave in the afternoon for Kansas City so will drive from there to Lawrence for the Conference Spring meeting. Will be home Saturday night.

On Sunday, Mother and I will go to Washington and then NY for a week. I'm glad Mom can go with me. I have a lot to do, but I'm sure she'll enjoy herself.

I think it would be good to all read the same books and discuss them this summer. Why don't you let me know which ones you have in mind? Maybe I can do some reading while traveling in case I get real busy later on.

I haven't had time to play much golf, but am developing a fine mental attitude for the Wichita journey. With my handicap, I'll be as tough as Palmer!!

It will be wonderful to have you home. I'm truly looking forward to the summer. Good luck in your exams—and don't worry.

All my love, always,
Dad

The second semester of my freshman year at Duke was coming to a close. With the conclusion of spring practice, and perhaps thanks to the distraction of Joe College Weekend, I rallied in the classroom. For me, it would be another excellent semester academically, and I looked forward to discussions at home on lessons learned in my history, English, political science, and religion classes.

College athletic programs like Oklahoma football, then and now, and Duke basketball today, have transcended their original purpose of providing an avenue to develop fully the mind and body of the student athlete. The support and encouragement Dad was given at OU was due in large part to the university administration's desire to build a "name" program, one that would attract attention to the institution as a whole. And it worked. Not only did his success help the university begin to market itself; it also created a strong brand identity: Oklahoma Sooners.

Dad understood the importance of the brand. Every recruit with whom he came into contact was made to understand what it meant to be a Sooner. In fact, at halftime of the Colorado game in Boulder in 1956 during OU's record forty-seven straight wins, Dad was so frustrated by his team's poor performance that he told his players to remove their jerseys, as he deemed them unworthy of the privilege of wearing the school's colors. He then turned and left the locker room. Before the team returned to the playing field, he built up their confidence, and they rallied to win and maintain the winning streak.

In that respect Dad was already an astute businessman, and he understood that he would have to create awareness of and interest in the President's Council on Fitness. He had both to create a message and to determine how that message would be communicated to the population at large. He was acutely aware of the importance of advertising to stimulate interest in his newest endeavor, and he got to work actively engaging that resource. Through his efforts, the Advertising Council, made up of representatives of the nation's most successful advertising agencies, became the Fitness Council's biggest asset. Professional marketers designed a national media campaign to promote the importance of a fit and active lifestyle. Ultimately, the ads and their placement were provided at no cost to the American taxpayer. The message saturated the marketplace, and its visibility was a critical factor in the Fitness Council's overall success.

During our high school years, Pat and I always tried to get summer jobs in construction because the physically demanding nature of the work helped keep us in shape. After wrapping up final exams in Durham, I headed back to Norman comfortable in the knowledge I had once again landed a spot on a construction crew. I looked forward to working side by side with one of my very best friends, Gary Rawlinson, whose father, Ken, was OU's head football trainer.

Our employer, Manhattan Construction, had contracts to build two state office buildings adjacent to the State Capitol in Oklahoma City. Gary and I pushed deep wheeled barrels filled with concrete, known as "Georgia buggies," down long wooden ramps and emptied them for the finishing crews to smooth with their bull floats and hand floats. It was excellent exercise because the concrete had to be moved quickly before it hardened, which meant you had to push a heavy load with speed. The temperature was hovering around the century mark, and that helped me adjust to similar temperatures when I returned for Duke's fall football practice.

I respected the men with whom I worked, including "Big John," who preached the importance of hard work, discipline, and doing what was expected. He reminded me a lot of my dad. But I also knew I did not want to do that kind of manual labor for the rest of my life. Construction work both hardened the body and strengthened my resolve to complete my education and do something meaningful with my life, preferably out of the hot Oklahoma sun. The summer shot by. The football season was fast approaching and Dad and I both did our best to prepare for it. When his first letter arrived during my sophomore year, the season was well under way.

PART II

Sophomore Year

1961–1962

> Hard work and togetherness, they go hand in hand. You
> need the hard work because it's such a tough atmosphere
> . . . to win week in and week out. You need togetherness
> because you don't always win and you gotta hang tough.

> Tony Dungy, Super Bowl–winning coach

Dad was not the only one writing letters to me at college. My
mother was a major influence in my life, too, and a source of great
comfort, understanding, and love.

Mom grew up as Mary Shifflett. Born and raised in Grinnell,
Iowa, as the second daughter to Grace and Glenn Shifflett, she
attended Carleton College for two years. It was there that she
met Dad. In addition to being an All American on the University
of Minnesota's national championship football team, Dad was
the goalie on the hockey team. My parents first met following a
hockey game between Carleton and Minnesota. A rumor had
been floating among the Gopher hockey players that there was a
lovely "Indian princess" on the Carleton campus. She turned out
to be my mom. When the time came for her to meet her date that
evening, she found the entire Gopher team in her sorority lobby.
She was surprised and embarrassed. When Mom later transferred
to Minnesota, she and Dad began to date. They were married in
1938 and moved to Syracuse, New York, where Dad was earning
his master's degree as a graduate assistant coach. Two years later
my brother Pat was born, and I came along in 1942.

Mom was a woman of beauty, style, and grace. She always made others feel welcomed in our home. Most assistant coaches and their wives had children, and she made them feel comfortable in any situation. As players' wives were allowed to travel with the team during bowl games, she organized private events to assure that they felt included during those special occasions.

My mother complemented Dad in many ways. They lit up a room whenever they entered together. She was kind and soft spoken, and since Dad traveled a great deal, she took great care of my brother and me when he was away. She cooked wonderful meals, kept the house immaculate, and encouraged her husband and sons in all our pursuits. Pat and I believe that whatever credit or blame goes to our parents for the way we turned out in life, much of the impulse for good derived from our mother.

Gung Ho Spirit

10/4/1961—Tuesday

Dear Jay,

It was good to get your letter. I think it's fine you are now going to be a swing end. It should be a great position for you. Unless I miss my guess you will also be playing quite a bit of safety before long.

I hate to be discouraged about our team, but frankly, I am. We no longer have the real "Gung Ho" spirit—and without it a team can't do very well. I don't think I'm doing a decent job of coaching either—but I'm trying to.

Somehow I feel I'm not getting through to our team like I should. Unless I can uncover the problem and correct it—we won't play well again.

Our Iowa State game is vital. If we lose this one—I doubt if we can win a single game all year. The way we practiced tonight—I doubt if we will win—but I'm going to do my best—and I hope the team will too.

We will be looking for you on December 20. I'm sorry too it is so late—but we'll more than make up for it.

Lots of luck Saturday.

> Love always,
> Dad

As the 1961 college football season got under way the fortunes at Oklahoma and Duke had reversed since the two teams had tangled in the Orange Bowl at the conclusion of the 1957 campaign. While Dad was coming off his first losing season, Duke came into the autumn as the defending ACC champion. Hopes were high in Durham. Such was not the case in Norman.

It was still somewhat strange to read Dad's concerns about not connecting with his team and hard to imagine any of his players not delivering their best under any circumstance. For those of us closest to my father, he never hid his humanity, never sugarcoated any subject. Although he put forth an attitude of confidence and strength in his duties as head coach, behind closed doors he could be vulnerable. Just as I had been in my freshman year, I was worried about him, but this time I felt I might have good reason to be worried.

His team began the season losing at Notre Dame. The next week, in the game that Dad thought was critical for his team's fortunes, OU fell at home to Iowa State 21–15. The Sooners would then drop their third in a row to Texas in Dallas to fall to 0–3. My father's worst fears were being realized.

I returned to Duke for my sophomore year still listed as the number seven quarterback on the depth chart. I had slowly resigned myself to the likelihood that I would be a redshirt, practicing with the team but destined to see no game action, in order to preserve my sophomore year of eligibility. During our final scrimmage the week before Duke's opening game against South Carolina, one of our great athletes, Ed Chesnutt, a fine receiver from Charlotte and the starting catcher on the baseball team, suffered a season-ending knee injury. Because players played both ways, depth was critical, especially at a position like receiver, where athletes ran pass routes or positioned themselves for downfield blocking on almost every offensive play, and then had to play defense. In Duke's scheme, three receivers saw plenty of action. With Chesnutt out for the year, I asked Coach Murray if I could try out as a receiver, and I earned the job. Chesnutt's misfortune became my good fortune, because as the seventh-team quarterback, I would otherwise never have played that year.

Duke opened its season on the road with a narrow 7–6 victory over South Carolina. I did not play in that game, but by the time week two rolled around I was named the team's number-two punt returner. Against Virginia in Richmond, I made my varsity debut. Late in the second quarter I dropped back in punt-return formation as Duke's single safety. After catching the ball I wove my way toward the sideline, where I suddenly had a wall of blockers in front of me and dashed untouched into the end zone for a sixty-three-yard punt return. The first time I touched the ball as a Blue Devil, I scored. We went on to rout the Cavaliers 42–0.

The next week in our home opener, we topped Wake Forest to lift our record to 3–0, a far cry from Oklahoma's 0–3 mark. The fact that Dad was already looking forward to Christmas was telling. I knew that in his heart he feared 1961 would be a very long year.

◆〜◆

The Action Is So Fast

10/27/1961—Tuesday

Dear Jay,

We enjoyed your letter. The films often give you a different picture of plays than you remember. The action in a game is so fast—and reactions are so spontaneous—that part of the time you actually have a wrong impression of what was a good or bad play.

Ronnie Payne tore the cartilage in his knee working out in sweat clothes last Monday. I hate to keep talking about injuries, but it is almost unbelievable how many things have happened this year.

In many ways we have had our best week of practice of the entire year. If we can keep Colorado from hitting long passes or making a break-away run—I firmly believe we will win.

The house is so torn up it's almost unbelievable, but it will be lovely when it is finished. By next week we should have the furniture back in the living room and sun room.

Norman won again last night, but Chickasha held them 8 to 8 at the half and was in the game until late in the 4th quarter.

It's hard to believe FB will be over in only five weeks. We're going to try to rally and finish strong.

Will be pulling for you tomorrow, and will look forward to talking to you Saturday.

> All my love, always,
> Dad

By the time Dad wrote this letter, OU's record had fallen to 0–4 with an additional loss to Kansas, and he seemed nearly crestfallen with the injury to senior end Ronnie Payne. During the glory years of the late forties and the fifties, when one player fell to injury, Dad could insert another of almost equal talent. Such was not the case by 1961 as the Sooners' "air of invincibility" had nearly vanished. Yet, in his mind, each week provided new challenges and new opportunities, and that was what he had always been able to instill in his teams.

Despite my father's optimism, the Sooners lost at home to Colorado 22–14 to go winless through the first half of the year. As a head coach, he had had his teams go undefeated during four seasons and had lost no more than one game in ten of his first twelve seasons. Now Dad had dropped nine out of ten games dating to the second half of the 1960 season. This was indeed uncharted territory for him, and not only as a head coach. In his three years of varsity football at the University of Minnesota, the Golden Gophers won three national championships, going 8–0, 8–0, and 7–1 under legendary coach Bernie Bierman.

And then, at perhaps the lowest point of his coaching career, Dad did something that surprised everyone. On his weekly Sunday afternoon television show he told viewers that his team would win the remainder of its games! He stated this to viewers as matter-of-factly as any other evaluation he had made through the years. His prediction may have seemed foolhardy to many, considering that the second half of the Sooners' schedule included the likes of Missouri, Army, and Nebraska. And no team had ever lost five straight games and then won its next five.

Dad and I discussed on the telephone his decision to go public with his prediction. He had seen his team make progress over the first half of the year, and he thought forecasting success would generate added confidence for his players—and I agreed. Through the years, Dad's enormous success had been predicated on his ability to remind his teams consistently that if they were not mentally and emotionally prepared, failure was a distinct possibility. As his players prepared to enter the second half of their 1961 season, Dad's challenge was to bolster the confidence and expectations of his team in a positive direction, and so he took a 180-degree turn in his approach. Would it work?

⋖⊱∞⊰⋗

Sink the Navy

11/11/1961—Saturday A.M.

Dear Jay,

I am writing hurriedly to enclose an article from the *St. Louis Globe-Democrat* about the White House Conference. I thought you'd be interested.

Will be pulling for you to "sink the Navy" and will look forward to talking to you tonight.

Love,
Dad

Not every one of Dad's letters was filled with deep sentiment or fervent conviction. Sometimes he could only find the time to drop me a quick note. As I received this letter, I knew he was working as hard at coaching as at any time in his career. In the preceding week that work had paid off, as the Sooners defeated Kansas State 17–6 for their first victory of the year. The letter came from the Sooners' team hotel in Columbia, Missouri, written just hours before Oklahoma squared off against the formidable Mizzou Tigers, who were ranked in the top ten nationally. That Dad had clipped the newspaper article and sent it to me said plenty about his ability to compartmentalize his life.

He continued to devote time as well to his work at the helm of the President's Council on Fitness and, as a member of the Kennedy Administration, was eager to keep up with other important political matters of the day. In another article he shared from the *St. Louis Globe-Democrat*, he reported on how administration officials had attempted to sell the local public on one of their new policies, efforts that had failed to engender the hoped-for response. Political Editor March Clark opined, "If the Administration intended to use the conference as a means of brainwashing the public to any extent, it failed. . . . If the panel members go back to Washington and attempt to report to President Kennedy on what people at the grass root are thinking, they had better know how to write fiction." Clark's article was a sobering reminder that politics could be as tough an endeavor as college football.

That same morning, my Duke teammates and I were preparing for the Oyster Bowl, a traditional midseason clash played in Norfolk, Virginia, and arranged by the local Shrine temple. Given the presence of the mammoth Norfolk Naval Shipyard in nearby Portsmouth, Virginia, the Navy Midshipmen had become an Oyster Bowl fixture. Duke had met Navy once before in the contest, losing 40–7 in 1954.

The winning ways of my Blue Devil teammates and me had ended, after our 3–0 start, with consecutive defeats at the hands of Georgia Tech and Clemson. We had rebounded in week six of the season, knocking off North Carolina State 17–6 in a game in which I returned a punt eighty-two yards for a score and established a school record for most punt-return yards in a game.

With a 5–2 record, Navy was favored and bent on avenging our shocking upset of the Midshipmen the season before. In the first quarter, our quarterback, Walt Rappold, fired a seventy-seven-yard touchdown pass to me, my first scoring reception at Duke and the third touchdown of my sophomore season. That opened the scoring, and by day's end Duke prevailed 30–9.

That afternoon in Columbia, Missouri, Dad's Sooners triumphed 7–0 in a tenacious defensive struggle. As I was to learn later, the real struggle for my Dad had actually begun in a midweek practice. Through the years Dad always stressed that the alternate team was every bit as important as the first team, since both units played approximately the same amount of time. At OU, while the starters were the first team, the alternates were considered "1A."

During the Wednesday practice prior to the Missouri game, Dad had grown impatient with the attitude, discipline, and character of his alternate team. Before the end of practice he called the unit together and informed them he was demoting the group to "last" team, which amounted to fourth team, given the restricted size of travel squads of that time. And he meant it.

Alternate-team player John Tatum, an outstanding offensive

center and defensive linebacker, laughed when recounting the story decades later. He said when he was ready to board the bus in the customary manner of sitting with the first team, he was met by Gomer Jones, Dad's loyal assistant coach, who told him that the alternate team, now the "last" team, was to ride on the second bus. When Tatum asked Gomer why, Jones responded, "Coach Wilkinson does not want you guys negatively influencing the first team." Tatum went on with the story: "When we arrived at the airport there were two DC3s, and we once again were told to travel on the second plane. When we arrived at the hotel we were placed in a separate wing and did not eat with the first team. Everything was segregated."

When OU lost the toss and Missouri elected to receive the ball, Dad told the alternate-team players that losing the coin flip was their fault! Missouri took the ball and drove to the OU 4-yard line, and Dad called a time-out. He gathered the alternate team around him and said: "This is your fault. Our first team has worked tirelessly but you have not paid the price! I don't want our first team to be scored on because they have tried so hard. Now you go in and let Missouri score on you!"

As Tatum remembers, the alternate team was so fired up that the unit could have stopped the Green Bay Packers! They made a valiant stand and kept Missouri out of the end zone. OU would hold the Tigers scoreless all afternoon, and the Sooners were two wins into the five-game streak Dad had promised the entire state.

November 11, 1961, marked the first time Dad and I both emerged victorious on the same day. There had been a lot of winning in our household over the years, but I do not believe any day was sweeter than that day when Duke claimed an Oyster and OU took the Tigers by the tail.

A Most Memorable Year

11/29/1961—Wednesday

Dear Jay,

We are just finishing our mimeographing of all the game preparations for Oklahoma State. Knowing it's the last time this year—in a way, makes me sad. Of course in other ways it's good because I'll have so much more free time.

If we win Saturday, I'll consider this a most memorable year. Our team has shown great courage to come back. It would be a shame to lose now when we could finish so well.

Mother is like a little girl she's so excited about her trip. She's still worrying about your not doing what you want to on Saturday night! Really you should. I know you will.

I'll be listening for the Notre Dame score. You've had a fine year—truly tremendous—and I hope you can climax it with another breakaway run.

Christmas will be so much fun. It will be wonderful to see you soon. Good luck, Saturday.

> All my love,
> Dad

By the time I received this letter, Dad had pulled off the nearly impossible, making good on his prediction that his team would win the last five games of the season. Many people, including ex-players and fellow coaches, considered the second half of the 1961 season to be his finest hour as a coach. Just as the first half of the year had been agonizing for him, he remembered to have fun while guiding his troops over the five-game win streak.

Dad always enjoyed surprises and throughout his coaching career he was well known for pulling tricks against the opposition. At Yankee Stadium in his team's November 18 showdown against Army, Dad knew the Cadets had a tendency to form their defensive huddle far away from the line of scrimmage and then to get into position slowly. He designed a trick play in which Jimmy Carpenter quickly took the quarterback snap after being tackled and then, before Army could get settled in defensively, pitched the ball to Mike McClellan, who ran seventy-five yards for OU's first score of the day. That play made the difference in the Sooners' 14–8 victory.

The next week against Nebraska at Lincoln, yet another side of Dad's coaching genius emerged. With OU down 14–0 at halftime, Dad entered the locker room and, according to Leon Cross, who would become a team co-captain and all-conference player in 1962, told his team that their character could not fill up a thimble. Cross said it was the first time he had ever heard Dad criticize individual players by name. When the officials came to the locker room for the five-minute warning, Dad told Gomer, in a voice loud enough to be heard by the entire squad, "I don't want to be seen with these men. It's an embarrassment! I'm going to get a head start and you bring them out for the second half." Ronnie Payne, recovered from his injury, stood up and shouted, "Let's go kick their ass!" Dad swung around and said, "Sit down and shut up, Ronnie! That's the problem with this team. You are all talk and no action." According to John Tatum, "You could have heard a pin drop."

His strategy worked to perfection. The Sooners scored 21 second-half points and pulled off a miraculous 21–14 come-from-behind victory over the Cornhuskers. Dad knew just the right moment to challenge his players in a manner opposed to his usual soft-spoken and affirming style. The team's remarkable four-game win streak proved his coaching convictions as much as or more than all his championship seasons. In the face of adversity, he not only regained his connection to his players but was also willing to take great risks that they would respond to his leadership style with dedication and courage.

After we indeed "sank the Navy," Duke knocked off North Carolina 6–3 in Durham to win the Atlantic Coast Conference championship. During that game I almost cost our team the win by trying to field a punt that hung in the air just a tad too long. A North Carolina player never broke stride and hit me just as the ball touched my hands; he knocked me back five yards in the air. Fortunately, our team rallied from that fumble and held Carolina to only a field goal, preserving the victory.

While Dad was concluding the season with a 21–13 home win over Oklahoma State for a fifth straight victory, Mom traveled to Durham for Duke's final game against Notre Dame. It was exciting to have her in attendance, although she was always unbearably nervous before football games. It was her second time that season to see the Fighting Irish play. Notre Dame had opened the year with a 19–6 win over Oklahoma. My teammates and I gained a measure of revenge for my father. I caught a twelve-yard touchdown pass and Duke throttled Notre Dame 37–13.

For someone who had begun fall practice as a seventh-team quarterback, my sophomore season had turned out remarkably well. Our team finished the year with a 7–3 record, beginning and ending with three-game win streaks. In addition to playing significant minutes as a lonesome-end and defensive halfback, I finished the season as the nation's second leading punt returner behind the great Lance Alworth of Arkansas. Every time I took the field that year, I considered that if not for the misfortunate of an injured teammate, I would never have had the opportunity to play.

Throughout the season Dad never lost faith in his team or in me—although to motivate them, he knowingly challenged some of his players to think otherwise in the Missouri and Nebraska games. He balanced his responsibility as both a coach and a father—and successfully provided encouragement, inspiration, and focus for positive results.

Pat and I were not the only ones who received letters and counsel from our dad. Once a year he would meet with each of his players individually to review academic and athletic performance and to provide motivational insight. Depending on the situation, he would sometimes write personal notes to his players, just as he sent letters to Pat and me.

On one occasion when Dad learned that Ronnie Payne was having trouble with his grades, in large part due to the team's performance on the field, he called Ronnie into his office. At the end of the meeting Dad gave him a framed copy of the poem "The Man in the Glass," which stresses the importance of being true to yourself.

The next week during the Christmas break Ronnie received a letter from Dad saying he had thought about their discussion and wanted Ronnie to read a book he had sent with the letter: *The Listener*, by Taylor Caldwell. Ronnie said: "The book illustrates what it is to have someone listen to you and to understand there are many people with problems more critical than yours. It was a great personal help to me at a difficult time in my life. I made my grades, graduated, and played pro ball. Coach Wilkinson's taking time to write and send me that book during a difficult time was a key part of my success."

I believe Charley Mayhue, a fine halfback from Ada, Oklahoma, summed it up best when he said, "Other than my father and the good Lord Jesus, Bud had as much influence on me as anybody. When I was around him, I felt a feeling of security and greatness. I felt inspired to do things more than I really had the capability of doing. He could get the best out of players when the first person you have to defeat is yourself.

"To be able to defeat yourself, when you're fatigued and keep it ongoing; when you're discouraged and keep it ongoing; when everybody else is complaining and you don't complain. You get the best out of your abilities that you can."

I was taught the same thing. Whether I was seventh-team Duke quarterback or Duke receiver and punt returner, Dad's inspiration, love, and support instilled in me the same kind of confidence Charley Mayhue described. It made a profound difference in my performance that season.

⟨∗⟩

The Value of Education

January 4, 1962

Dear Jay,

It was wonderful having you home for Christmas. The time always seems to pass too rapidly, and we become so engrossed in inconsequential things that we often fail to talk over the realities of life.

The poet Wordsworth said it better. "The world is too much with us late and soon. Getting and spending we lay waste our powers. Little we see in nature that is ours."

I know that academic work is particularly difficult when goals and objectives are not clearly defined. Pat, wanting to study medicine, can see cause and purpose in the courses he is taking. You, not knowing what your goals are, find it, naturally enough, extremely difficult to see the validity in much of what you're asked to do.

Education in the final analysis is simply the development of self-discipline of the mind. James Conant, former President of Harvard, once remarked, "Your education is what you have left after you have forgotten all that you learned."

If you can bear down hard on your studies and do well in them even though you do not have a great deal of interest in them, think of how simple and easy it will be to do well when you are highly motivated and truly enjoy the work.

I know what a sense of commitment and dedication you have concerning your future life. I'm also convinced that in due time your course will become clear. If you live each day well, the future takes care of itself.

All my love, always,
Dad

PS: Good luck in your exams. Don't worry—just do your best.

Dad's quotes from the poet William Wordsworth and the former Harvard president James Conant demonstrated not just a well-read mind but an ease with bringing things other than football into his everyday dialogue. Following the heart-stopping excitement of my first year of formal college football, I returned from Christmas vacation and immediately headed back to reality: the always dreaded semester-ending final examinations. As a coach, Dad was well aware of the academic challenges facing every student-athlete, particularly those of a football player whose season contained so many physical, mental, and emotional obstacles. His encouragement for me to do my best inspired me to do just that.

Dad was committed to the idea that the primary reason athletes were in school was to receive a college degree. He was exceedingly proud that his players graduated from OU at a rate of almost 90 percent. Today many top-flight football programs are fortunate to graduate half their student-athletes. While many of Dad's players went on to play professionally and some would make a living as high school, college, and professional coaches, many more carved out their livelihoods, established careers, and became well known for their business achievements based on their educational pursuits at the University of Oklahoma.

In 1949 Oklahoma Memorial Stadium was expanded to a seating capacity of fifty-five thousand. In the process, the north end of the stadium was enclosed and the school's athletic offices were relocated there. In addition, the university's world-renowned Department of Architecture moved its operations from the old Navy Air Station on Norman's north side to the stadium, one floor removed from the football offices.

I was not yet eight years old when Dad gave me a tour of the stadium's improvements. As we walked up to the new "front doors" of Owen Field, he noticed two large signs at the entrance to the stadium. One read: "OU Department of Athletics." Below it was another sign that said: "OU Department of Architecture." Dad was noticeably upset by what he saw. Thinking aloud, he told me the signs had to be reversed to place the academic sign *above* the athletic sign. A short time later the change was made. The move was consistent with and symbolic of his beliefs about the importance of education.

⟨⋙⋘⟩

Excellence

January, 1962

Dear Jay,

As a golfer, I find myself disappointed and encouraged. I've played four times. I've hit the ball well most of the time, but have been most inconsistent around the greens. The first round I played I four putted two greens the first 9 holes. Believe me, this makes it a little difficult to hold the putter with confidence!!

I keep thinking I'm going to play well and my stroke feels quite solid—but I miss just enough shots to keep myself from scoring well. The challenge of the game never ends—I guess that's why it's so much fun to play.

We've slept about 10 hours every night. I didn't think I could sleep so much—but when you are away from cares and responsibility it's surprising how easy it is to sleep.

I had planned to work hard on our football offense and defense for next year. My schedule was supposed to be study in the morning, golf in the afternoon. Up to now I've slept too late and haven't accomplished much. Although deadlines are nerve-wracking, they do provide a real stimulus to activity. Most of us need some sort of schedule to work with full effectiveness. Self-discipline is still one of the most difficult qualities to achieve.

I've read two most interesting books—*The Status Seekers*—and *Excellence*. Both are on somewhat the same theme. *The Status Seekers* analyzes the problems of class distinctions in the U.S. The sense of "belonging" and also the urge to better one's self provide the drives and frustrations of status seeking. The author fears—and I'm afraid with justification—that America is becoming a somewhat rigid society of distinct classes.

Excellence examines how this needed quality excellence—can best be developed in our kind of society. The inter-relationship of hereditary privilege, egalitarianism, and competitive performance in America are analyzed. All are a part of our social structure and we believe in—and practice—all of them. For example, socially we are class conscious—Educationally we believe in equal opportunity—Economically we are for competition. What we sorely need is a means of providing equal educational opportunity for all—reward talent and performances, while protecting those incapable of competing well—

and accepting the worth of individuals on character—not technical proficiency. This is a most difficult goal for any society. Proper education could bring it into reality. Only through education will men push aside selfish interest—recognize the importance of "giving to" not "getting from" the world.

Right now, you're in the midst of exams. I know the fine effort you're making—and I'm with you in spirit and heart all the way.

All my love, always,
Dad

PS: If you took my beautiful, good handkerchiefs with you when you left for school, please buy some and send mine back. They were gifts from Ethel and the Sneeds and I can't replace them as they all came from Switzerland.

The letter was written from the Gran Hotel Ancira in Monterrey, Mexico. Mom and Dad were secluded in a relaxed environment where he could enjoy two of his favorite recreational activities: golf and study. Such occasions provided a proper balance to achieve both objectives, and it was a similar experience to their trip a year earlier to Eldorado Beach in Puerto Rico. Under such coaching pressure, it was important to have an outlet in order to get away and gain a more measured perspective on life.

Dad's observations regarding *The Status Seekers* and *Excellence* were insightful, and his comments regarding society and the class system evidence issues with which our country continues to grapple today. His ceaseless efforts to better himself intellectually and his willingness to take the time to summarize and offer conclusions about both books instilled in me a desire to emulate those qualities.

Although Dad was always disinclined to name his favorite

players, over the years he was particularly proud of two individuals who came through his program: Prentice Gautt, the first African American to play football at Oklahoma, and Jakie Sandefer, a child of privilege who was one of the hardest-working and most passionate players ever to wear a Sooners uniform.

Gautt, an Oklahoma City native and a product of all-black Douglass High School, officially broke OU's color barrier in 1957. Often during his three years at Oklahoma, he was forced to stay in hotel accommodations other than those reserved for the team. I am sure he faced many other challenges of which he rarely or never spoke. Yet he seemed always to have a smile on his face, and during my years in high school, Gautt was a player for whom I had enormous respect.

Sandefer, on the other hand, was a firebrand. His real name was Jefferson Davis Sandefer III and his father, J.D., was a wealthy oil operator from Breckinridge, Texas. Named for the president of the Confederate States of America, Jakie came from a family whose loyalties in the aftermath of the Civil War were not difficult to imagine. But in the late 1950s at OU, Jakie and Prentice were teammates, friends, and roommates on road trips. Despite their contrasting life histories, they treated each other, and the rest of their teammates, with dignity and respect.

In many respects, Prentice and Jakie were the consummate "Wilkinson men." Both were positive role models as players and later in life. Gautt went on to play in the National Football League, then proceeded to earn his doctoral degree and become assistant commissioner of the Big Eight Conference. Jakie followed his father's lead and made a career in the oil business, heading up Sandefer Oil and Gas Company for many years.

As for the handkerchiefs my father mentioned in his postscript, I stand today guilty as charged. He valued those gifts from his stepmother Ethel and friends Earl and Cornelia Sneed. Earl had been dean of OU's law school and the university's faculty representative to both the Big Seven and Big Eight conferences. In addition, he and Cornelia were close friends of my parents. The sentimental value, not to mention the quality of those fine pieces of silk, made the handkerchiefs prized accessories in my father's wardrobe. Rest assured, they were immediately returned.

⊲⊱⋅⋅⋆⋅⋅⊰⊳

Conviction

2/5/1962—Saturday A.M.

Dear Jay,

Mom and I returned yesterday from New Orleans. Keith had asked me to speak at a Layman's Leadership Institute. There were about 800 in attendance, and I felt out of place. Most of the men are Southern Baptist. I don't mean this critically, but I don't understand, in depth, their theology. I do envy their conviction. Keith thought my talk was all right, but I believe he was and is most prejudiced.

I keep extremely busy without accomplishing much. At the office the phone rings, people stop by, the coaches come in to talk. Very little constructive gets done. Actually, if I could be here at home I'd make much more rapid progress.

Pat writes that he'll be home March 21st. I hope you'll be here about that time. We'll try to plan a few fun things to do.

I'll be interested in how Spring Practice goes. Write when you've time and let me know. Mother joins in sending our love.

As always,

Dad

A lifelong member of the Episcopal Church, Dad held Southern Baptists, Oklahoma's largest denomination, in high regard. Many of the state's most powerful and influential business leaders were Baptists, and Dad had great respect for their religious conviction and history of coming to the aid of the less fortunate or those in dire need. He knew that conviction made an enormous difference in people's outlook on life and their contributions to society. He also knew that conviction made a huge difference in the character of his football players and was a major factor in his teams' successes.

Dad spoke to the Layman's Leadership Institute in New Orleans at the request of Keith Miller, today a well-known author of several books on religious and spiritual issues. Miller was a close friend of my father's who taught the adult Bible study class at our family's church, St. John's Episcopal Church in Norman. Dad and Keith spent many hours in our home discussing matters of theological significance. Knowing my dad to be a spiritual man, Keith had encouraged him to accept the invitation to the institute. It was not lost on either Miller or my father that the majority of members of the institute were Southern Baptists.

At times Dad became weary of the requirements and expectations of organized religion, including the precepts of the Southern Baptist denomination. He believed such matters as smoking, drinking, dancing, and gambling were at worst minor moral issues that did not fully shape a person's character. While accepting of these activities in others, Dad held himself to a high standard of personal conduct as a respected leader. He placed little significance on biblical interpretation that he called "micro-ethics" but held in high regard the emphasis the Gospels place on mercy, as taught in the parables of the Prodigal Son and the Good Samaritan, and other New Testament stories of compassion and understanding. Throughout his life, he stood firm in his belief that there was no better historical role model for living to be found in any world religion than that of Jesus Christ.

⋖⋗⋖⋗

Improving Chances

February 7, 1962

Dear Jay,

Enclosed you will find your tax card and your withholding slips. I believe you should fill out the form and mail it soon. You should get a refund as I am quite sure more money has been withheld than you owe in taxes.

Mother and I had planned to go to Phoenix this week prior to the FB Clinic at Los Angeles, but I seemed to be a little behind on our recruiting and thought I'd better visit with some boys and their parents.

So far things seem to be coming along quite well. As always four or five critical boys will make the difference, but I feel we have a better chance to have a fine freshman team than has been the case for many years.

Larry Shields visited last week and told me you had written. He appreciated your letter, and I know it helped us. He told me he thought he would come to OK but wanted to make a couple more visits before making up his mind for sure. He is supposed to be an excellent player. I do hope he'll come here.

I know you're getting ready for spring practice. I hope everything will go well for you, and I believe it will. Be sure and work out enough to be in excellent condition. It is a physical contest, as you know, and there is no substitute for strength, speed, and endurance.

I hope to see you the later part of the month. As yet my plans are a bit indefinite. As soon as I know when I will be coming East I'll write or call.

Mother joins me in sending our love.

As always,
Dad

After Dad's two most challenging and difficult seasons, recruiting was his highest priority. Although there was talk throughout the coaching fraternity of a return to two-platoon football, as Dad traveled the recruiting trail in the early months of 1962, he continued to look for the same type of young man who had helped him build his championship program. These were players who not only possessed an overall athletic ability but also worked well within a system that emphasized discipline, learning, and strong moral character. Dad knew these were ingredients that helped maintain a team's cohesion and commitment to excellence.

After the Sooners' spectacular finish to the 1961 season, for the first time in two years my father felt he had some wind at his back. Just as the difference between winning and losing on the field was often a fine line, so it was in the recruiting wars. Just four or five key individuals could mean the difference between success and mediocrity on the gridiron. Larry Shields was one such key player. It meant a lot to me that I could do something constructive to help my dad's program, and I was pleased when Larry signed his letter of intent to play at Oklahoma, where he had a fine career as a halfback.

As Duke spring practice approached, with an abundance of quality players on the depth chart at quarterback, Coach Murray and his staff decided to move me from receiver to a running back position. Dad's encouragement for me to *begin* spring workouts in top physical shape meant that I would be able to excel from day one rather than spend time honing my body for the demands of the sport. In this case he was preaching to the choir, as he had long ago taught me the importance of excellent physical conditioning.

❧❦❧

Together in Spirit

2/17/1962

Dear Jay,

Thank you so much for your wonderful Valentine letter. While it is true that growing to maturity means a certain degree of separation—I can't believe we'll ever be too far from each other. I know we'll always see each other often—and even though we are apart, that we're always together in spirit.

This week's Clinic is a double header. Duffy, Royal, and Rogers talked here in Houston yesterday. Bryant, Gilstrap, and myself were in Dallas. Last night we flew here and they flew to Dallas to complete the Clinic at each place.

I've been gone so much. I'm truly anxious to get home and stay home. Next week I must be in Chicago Monday, Atlantic City, Tuesday, speak at the Navy FB Banquet Tuesday night—be in Washington for meetings Wednesday, Thursday, and Friday. I had hoped to get down to see you—I still am going to try—if I don't have to be back in Norman for recruiting on the weekend.

Mother loved her night gown—it was wonderful of you to remember to send it.

I hope practice is going well. I'm anxious to hear about it and will call you in a day or two.

All my love, always,

Dad

As a father, Dad easily articulated his love for his sons. I knew it was not common for men of his day to convey feelings of warmth and devotion to children so openly and directly, but the closing of all his letters gave testimony to the fact that he could not only express it but also really meant it in the truest and most noble sense of the word. His letters consistently show a very human side to a very iconic figure. His response to my Valentine letter to him and my mother indicates that it struck a chord about our deep bond, always together in spirit even when separated by distance.

While Pat and I both found physical closeness a more enjoyable state than spiritual closeness alone, the reality of my family's spiritual connection was important to me and sustained me while apart from my parents and brother. The depth of our love transcended geographic proximity, which was a good thing, since Pat was on one coast finishing up his undergraduate studies at Stanford, I was on the other coast, and our parents were in the heartland. With Dad's frequent travels, it seemed the four members of our family were indeed loving one another from afar more often than not.

Of particular interest in this letter is Dad's casual mention of his peers who assisted him with his Coach of the Year clinics. Several of those names belong in the pantheon of greatest college coaches of all time. Duffy Daugherty was Dad's principal partner in the clinic business. In early 1962 Daugherty was still three years away from his greatest coaching success, leading his Michigan State team to the 1965 national championship. In 1966 his Spartans tied with Notre Dame in a contest many called the "game of the century."

Darrell Royal of Texas and Bear Bryant of Alabama were legendary coaches as well. Royal was one of Dad's first standout players at OU, and when he defeated my father for the first time as a coach, it made Royal physically ill. He is famously remembered for having said of the Cotton Bowl triumph in 1958, "It just doesn't seem right to beat Coach Wilkinson." Unfortunately for Dad, Royal made beating OU a habit, besting him in the last six years of his coaching career. Bear Bryant and Dad were destined to cross paths competitively again at the conclusion of the 1962 season.

Clinics such as the one my dad ran successfully for many years, and which continue today in a variety of forms, were and are an anomaly in business. Coaches share with other clinic coaches the inner workings of their successful strategies in defense, offense, and special-teams play. They willingly and openly disclose all manner of techniques and philosophy that have given them an edge over opponents. This is in sharp contrast to the focus on confidentiality agreements and noncompete clauses in other kinds of businesses.

⟨⟩

Dad's Visit to Durham

2-26-1962

Dear Jay,

It was good to be with you. I was sorry the time was so short—but it was much better than not seeing you at all.

In my mind's eye, I had hoped to spend about three days—talk with you—play a little golf—look at your last year's games—and take your friends to dinner. Perhaps we can do it this way later in the year.

I was particularly pleased to meet your friends—but am sorry I didn't have a chance to talk with them more leisurely.

My trip home was uneventful. We had a rough flight—and were a couple of hours late, but I made it in time for dinner.

I thought you looked excellent in practice. I was so tired—I'm not sure I described well what I thought you could do to improve—but I do hope it was of some assistance. I'm only concerned about your lack of rest. During spring practice, I believe you should make every effort to get at least 8 hours sleep each night. When you're not working out—you can get by on six—but when you're in violent physical activity, you need the extra rest.

I am anxious to hear about the scrimmage—and also the party. I hope you did well, and am sure you did. I also hope the party was fun.

Mother was pleased and proud to learn of your election as President of FCA. I hope you'll send the clipping.

We love you so much and are looking forward to seeing you soon.

Love always,
Dad

Dad saw Duke play only a handful of times on national or regional television broadcasts during my college career. Yet during spring practice of my sophomore year of school, despite his busy schedule, he committed to paying me a visit in Durham. Roy Bostock had finished his football career at Duke, and I asked him to pick up my father at the airport.

As they sat together watching us go through a physically demanding practice at in Wallace Wade stadium, Roy said Dad told him, "We stopped doing that kind of work long ago at Oklahoma and do it only occasionally. We concentrate on speed and agility. Hitting is for games; you get too many injuries in practice." Roy said he sighed and with a grin responded, "Coach, I think I would have liked playing for you!"

Unfortunately, Dad was tired and feeling a little under the weather during his stay, so our time together was not quite what it normally was when we were reunited. Still, his presence made a lasting impression on many of my teammates. Biff Bracy, a half-back from Orangeburg, South Carolina, later told me, "One of my fondest memories was when your father came to Duke during spring practice. I have never forgotten the intensity and clarity of his eyes as he seemed to be interested in everything that we had to say. I remember his quiet demeanor and gentle spirit." I was only sorry there was not time for Dad to have known my teammates better.

With Duke's challenging academic requirements, I was again finding it difficult to balance the demands of the practice field with those of the classroom. While I was proud—and relieved—to be named to the dean's honor roll during the 1961 season, by the spring I was struggling to keep my academic marks up to that standard. My days began early and ended late, and as I tried my hardest to avoid burning the candle at both ends, the simple fact was that my dedication to my responsibilities and obligations meant that I was not getting enough sleep.

Few football players really enjoy spring practice. It is a time when coaches evaluate which players have the physical toughness and mental determination to play. The physical contact is violent and continues throughout the entire practice schedule. Later in our final spring practice I broke two left fingers on the first play of scrimmage—fortunately the only time I broke bones playing football.

My fellow Phi Delts who were both fraternity brothers and football teammates always marked their calendar with two of the biggest social events of the school year. The parties, one immediately after the final game of the regular season and the other after the final scrimmage of spring practice, symbolized that for those of us on the Blue Devil football team, physical contact was at an end, at least for a while, and this was clearly a very good thing. Dad had been involved in the Greek system at the University of

Minnesota, a member of the Psi Upsilon fraternity. Throughout his life he enjoyed a good time after an honest day's work, and we enjoyed comparing notes about our respective "extra-curricular" social activities while at school.

With spring practice over and some free time in my schedule, I added a new responsibility as president of the Duke chapter of the Fellowship of Christian Athletes. I believed then, as I do now, that FCA is one of the most worthwhile organizations in which any-one, of any age, can get involved. The FCA movement was born at Eastern Oklahoma State College in Wilburton, the inspiration of a young coach there by the name of Don McClanen. With the support and encouragement of one of baseball's legendary figures, Branch Rickey, McClanen obtained an official charter and non-profit status for the organization in 1954.

Port Robertson was OU's head freshman football coach and head wrestling coach. He had landed at Normandy on D-Day and received injuries that required hospitalization for six months, for which he received the Purple Heart. Port was Dad's "heavy," in charge of disciplining players who failed to attend class or make acceptable grades or who strayed too far from the righteous path of a Sooner sportsman. Former OU players are unanimous in their conviction that Robertson and assistant coach Gomer Jones were as important to the overall success of Dad's program as was the man in charge.

Port was a strict disciplinarian, but he was also a man of faith. He had become friends with McClanen and believed strongly in the FCA mission. With my father's assistance Port arranged for a campus visit by some of the biggest names in sports who also held strong Christian convictions. One of Dad's players, Chuck Bow-man, who later became Oklahoma director for the FCA, painted a vivid picture of that encounter.

"All the players and coaches were in the meeting room," Bowman said, "and soon the back door opened and in walks Coach Wilkinson and three other men. The first guy was wearing blue jeans, a blue jean jacket, and a small cowboy hat. He was small in stature and everyone thought he may have been the cab driver who brought the other men. The next guy we recognized right away as Otto Graham, the Cleveland Browns premier quarterback, who looked dignified in a three-piece suit. The third person looked a bit ragged, but we quickly learned he was an Oklahoma native, Pepper Martin, who was a member of the famous gashouse gang of the St. Louis Cardinals."

Bowman continued, "Coach Wilkinson told us these men came to encourage the team to be open to the FCA. Then we learned the first guy in blue jeans was not a taxi driver, but was Doak Walker, one of the best running backs of all time as a three-time All American at SMU and the pride of the Detroit Lions! We couldn't believe how small and handsome he was. Then the three men each gave a testimony of their faith that was very motivational and inspirational. Following the meeting Coach Wilkinson said that if any OU players wanted to attend the FCA summer conference in Estes Park, Colorado, he would help make it happen.

"As a result of that meeting nine OU players traveled to the FCA Summer Conference in Estes Park. All Americans Clendon Thomas and Bill Krisher were part of that group and volunteered to address churches and high schools following the conference during the remainder of their time at OU. Each of the nine men believes those experiences strengthened the 1956 Sooner team that never lost a game and was ranked number one that year in the polls."

Many Duke athletes were also members of the Fellowship of Christian Athletes, and my election to president of our chapter was a proud moment, both for me and for my parents. Like many of Dad's players who gave time to travel around the state of Oklahoma to witness their faith to high school groups, the Duke FCA chapter was active with speaking engagements throughout North Carolina.

⊰⊱

Seeing the Stars

3-16-1962

Dear Jay,

I hope you aren't so worried about your studies that the worry is interfering with your work. If you're doing your best—as I am sure you are—don't worry about what grades you make.

There is a fine quote from Ralph Waldo Emerson which is on point. "When it is dark enough, men see the stars." I'm sure you'll come out fine—and if you don't, you'll learn from the experience. So don't worry or fret!

Our practice has been fair. We have more ability than we've had for quite a while—but we'll be so young and inexperienced that we will have a tough time in our early games against Syracuse, ND and Texas. We'll know a lot more about the situation by the time you get home.

Mother and I will look forward to meeting you Friday night. It will be wonderful to have you home again.

Love always,
Dad

PS: I checked again on the Summer School Bulletin and found it has not been returned from the printers. I don't know what has caused the delay—but as soon as it's available—you're first on the list to receive one.

I was worried. During my sophomore year as my grade point average began to decline, I felt a responsibility to do my best and to excel in the classroom. Dad's quote from Ralph Waldo Emerson reminded me that it was only during times of despair and discouragement that individuals can understand hope and confidence. The quote was like a gift from my father. It helped me to put things into their proper perspective, and in doing so, I began to try to orchestrate my life toward the best possible outcome.

❦

Worry vs. Convictions

4-2-1962

Dear Jay,

It was a pure delight to have you home. As always, the time went much too fast, but before long school will be over and we'll be together for the summer.

I hope you won't worry about your grades. Worry, as you well know, doesn't help accomplish anything. It merely diverts your attention from the task at hand.

In making an effort to develop and realize your full capacities by vocabulary growth, and speed reading, etc., I believe you are showing great integrity of purpose. Time spent in such pursuits does not improve your grades at all, but you learn more in the process than when you memorize to get good grades. The fact that you realize this and work to satisfy your own convictions of what you need most is a sign of great maturity. These basics will help you more through your life than any single course you may be studying now.

Please let us know how your hand heals. It will be stiff for a while, but if you work on it in the proper manner it will be strong again before too long.

We all join in sending our love. Write when you've time.

As always,
Dad

PS: Hope the flight was fast, smooth, and pleasant. We miss you already!

It was always fun to return home during spring break. The camaraderie, conversations, laughter, and friendly golf and gin rummy games made the time pass too quickly. Dad's prediction that vocabulary and speed-reading pursuits outside the regular academic curriculum would ultimately be more valuable than academic courses was a diversion from my continued focus on grades. Final examinations remained a source of anxiety for me and were a common theme in my father's letters. This was one of the few areas where it proved difficult for me to put his counsel into practice.

⋘⋙

Evaluation

4-7-1962—Saturday

Dear Jay,

We're going to have our first real scrimmage this afternoon. In practice on Thursday McQuarters sprained an ankle and Pearce bruised a knee. Except for these injuries we're in good shape. I'm anxiously looking forward to this afternoon because we should be able to evaluate our men quite well on the basis of their play today.

We finally moved Van Burkleo to HB. He simply couldn't break himself of bad, deeply ingrained habits. I hope and believe he'll play better at the new position. He isn't the smartest signal caller I've seen—and not having to call plays should relieve him of many worries which he seemed unable to cope with.

Ethel is visiting us and Bill and Mary will be here sometime early in the week. She has been in Phoenix for a month and has a beautiful tan.

I played 9 holes yesterday afternoon and shot 40. Took 3 from the edge of the green on 13, 15, and 16, but did hit the ball well. Minnesota look out!!

I am pulling for Charlie in the Masters. Palmer was great yesterday and probably will win. When you analyze who Charlie beats, it gives you a true appreciation of his caliber as a player.

We miss you—but know it won't be long until summer.

All my love, always,
Dad

Dad was excited about his first spring-practice scrimmage when he could evaluate the talent of his players. It was positive news that injuries to key players were not as pervasive as in the previous two years. He had decided to move Bill Van Burkleo from quarterback to halfback. Bill had been a rival of mine in the 1960 Oklahoma All-State Game and a teammate in the Oil Bowl when our Oklahoma squad upset the Texas team in the annual bi-state clash in Wichita Falls, Texas. He was one of the most gifted and talented players of his time with great speed, quickness, and toughness.

It was easy to envision the golf holes Dad described on the OU course since I had caddied or played rounds with him there on many occasions while growing up in Norman. Charlie Coe was one of the greatest amateur golfers of all time. He was always Big Seven Conference champion during his years at OU. In 1949 and 1958 he won the prestigious U.S. Amateur championship, and in 1959 he finished as the tournament's runner-up to a collegiate player from Ohio State: Jack Nicklaus! During the 1961 Masters, Coe finished only one stroke behind Gary Player—the closest any amateur has come to winning the famed Green Jacket. While Dad thought Arnold Palmer would probably win in 1962, he hoped Charlie would play well, as he and his wife Liz were intimate family friends.

Dad was right. Palmer won the Masters in '62, but he had to survive a three-way playoff to do so.

⋘⋙

The Wisdom of Judgment

April 15, 1962

Dear Jay,

I wish you wouldn't worry so about your grades. What you learn is important—not what grades you make. I know you're learning a great deal—probably more than the majority of people who may make higher grades.

As you know, the Kennedys were strictly average students. Adm. Halsey finished in the bottom ¼ of his class at Annapolis. There are many similar examples. Remember, you're in College to learn which involves the development of proper values—and the wisdom of judgment which comes from a broad experience in many difficult subjects. The inter-relationship of facts and ideas—understanding of why things happen as they do—plus the ability to project into the future are the essentials of an educated man. The ability to parrot back facts for tests doesn't have any true lasting meaning.

Our practice this week has been a little poorer than before. I'm sure our men are tired. I'm hoping we'll pick up next week for the Alumni Game. We're going to try desperately to win. If we can, it will give us the confidence we need for our tough early schedule in the fall.

The Alumni have, always, a strong squad. Thomas, McDonald, and Coyle are as good pass receivers as any in the world. Boyd, Pierce, Garrett, Harrison, Ed Gray, Krisher, and Jim Harris are all active Pros. They'll have a fine team, but if we're organized well, we could win.

I hope you have a good time on the big weekends coming up. This too is part of your education. You should participate and enjoy it.

We'll be hoping all goes well as I'm sure it will.

Love always,

Dad

Over the years academicians and philosophers have disagreed about definitions of learning. I was intrigued that Dad's brief exposition of the word included only two components—the development of proper values and the wisdom of judgment. That was it. That was the basis of what he believed a person needed to learn while in college.

His notion reinforced two of his primary assumptions. The development of proper values helps a person understand the importance of focusing on others—not on oneself. In addition, wisdom of judgment comes from many different disciplines, and helps people understand why things happen, and assists them in acquiring skills that will be useful in the future. I later learned how important this is in all business endeavors.

His philosophy here has great meaning for individuals and group leaders and offers a different perspective than many other views on education. His examples of the academic records of the

Kennedys and Admiral Halsey helped me put my own grades into perspective. While my sophomore year had been a success on the football field, unfortunately I took a step backward in the classroom, falling off the dean's honor roll.

Because of my struggles, I decided to enroll in summer courses at OU during my time home from Duke. I did so in lieu of construction work, hoping that the extra credit I would take back with me to Durham would alleviate some of the course pressures I felt at school.

Mom and Dad in the early 1960s; they lit up a room whenever they entered it.

Dad, holding Pat and me, before he was deployed to the Pacific as a naval officer in World War II.

Pat and I enjoyed playing in our backyard in Minneapolis. This photo was taken in 1946, the year our family moved to Norman, Oklahoma.

Reading the funnies at the East-West Shrine Game in 1951 with Frank Gifford (*right*), future Hall of Fame and All American football player and sportscaster, and Pat Cannamela (*left*), also a University of Southern California player and All American. I would play in that game twelve years later.

Mom, Dad, Pat, and I stopped for a photo upon our arrival at the Hula Bowl in Honolulu in 1952. I would also play in that game twelve years later.

Dad, Pat, and I display our catch on a fishing trip in Canada in 1959. Courtesy Pat Wilkinson.

On the back of this photo Mom wrote: "TD first time he touches the ball in college." It was a sixty-three-yard punt return against Virginia in 1961.

Our family relaxing together at home during the holidays in 1962.

Duke head football coach Bill Murray (*right*) gets
congratulations from Johnny Roventini, the Philip Morris
"living mascot," for Duke's victory over Maryland in 1963.
Looking on with me is Chuck Walker (*center*), Duke football
captain and an All ACC Conference and twelve-year NFL
player.

Receiving an award before Duke's game against Navy during
my senior season in 1963, as reported by Hall of Fame
television broadcaster Jim Simpson (*left*). The Navy quarterback
was Roger Staubach, who won the Heisman Trophy that year.

With Dad at the 1963 *Look* All American awards
ceremony in New York City.

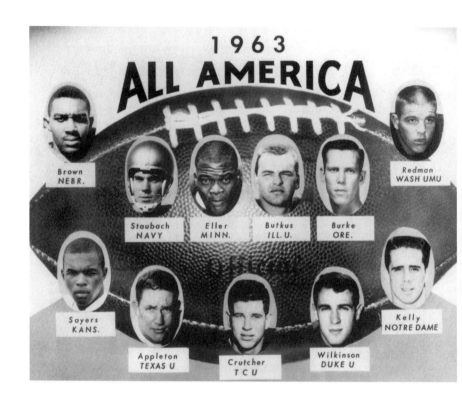

The 1963 American Football Coaches All American team.

Meeting with President Richard Nixon in 1969 when I was a
staff assistant to the president.

Pat and I posed with Dad for this photo at Pat's home in
Baltimore in 1991. Courtesy Pat Wilkinson.

PART III

Junior and Senior Years

1962–1963

> Inspiration exists, but it has to find us working.
>
> Pablo Picasso, Spanish painter and sculptor

I knew my sophomore year had been a good one, but I was not prepared for the fact that it landed me on the cover of the most famous college football yearbook of the day, *Street and Smith's*. I was more than a little embarrassed by the attention since I felt there were numerous seniors around the country, including several on my own team, who deserved the acclaim more than I did. Fortunately, my Duke teammates saw the exposure as good for the program and spared me from criticism, delivering only good-natured ribbing.

Certainly time spent in the college classroom had changed me too, expanding my knowledge, awareness, and curiosity about life's larger and more important issues. At the same time, I realized my studies were an element of my experience at Duke to date that continued to need sharp focus, and this helped me to justify my investment in summer school classes at OU.

Still, there was time for fun in the summer of '62, and for me, that time was split evenly between family and friends. Beyond the close father-son relationship I had with Dad, I had a strong friendship with my older brother Pat, and it was great to spend relaxed time with him during the summer. He had just graduated from

Stanford and would begin medical school at Johns Hopkins University in Baltimore.

Outside the family, both Pat and I spent much enjoyable time with Gary Rawlinson, Eddy Massey, Jerry Goldsby, Mike Martin, and other good friends with whom we felt comfortable and at ease. I also had a romantic friendship with Sue Ann White, daughter of Thurman White, dean of the OU Department of Continuing Education. All of these people excelled at OU and later in their personal and professional careers.

Among my classmates growing up from kindergarten through high school with whom I maintained close friendships were twins, Sherman and Steve Lawton. Their father, Dr. Sherman Lawton, and his wife Kathleen had migrated to Norman one year ahead of my parents when he became coordinator of broadcast instruction at OU. We lived within three blocks of each other.

The younger Sherman was valedictorian and president of our Norman High School senior class, while Steve was president of the student council. Later at OU Sherman became Phi Beta Kappa in his junior year; Steve was president of his senior class, the men's honor society PEET, and his Beta Theta Pi fraternity. Sherman later became a renowned neurologist affiliated with Baptist Hospital in Oklahoma City and helped care for Mom during her declining years. Steve had a distinguished law career as a partner with the international law firm Hogan and Hartson of Washington, D.C.

I came to appreciate the traditional American routine of the family dinner during the summer between my sophomore and junior years of college. As was customary, Dad was gone a good bit of the time that summer, delivering speeches around the country and making appearances on behalf of OU. Like most teenagers, I had taken for granted the significance and importance of eating with the family. I valued the time the four of us spent in one another's company since that time was more fleeting as the years went by.

Dad and I spent at least a small part of that summer ruminating about the possibility of our two teams meeting in the next Orange Bowl game. As Big Seven and ACC champions, Oklahoma and Duke had vied in the 1958 Orange Bowl. Given that *Street and Smith's* tabbed Duke as ACC favorites to repeat and the Sooners to battle Nebraska for league honors, the chance to be on the same field for that game seemed plausible and exciting to us both.

Dad knew the first two weeks of two-a-day football practices following my arrival at Duke would be strenuous and demanding, and his next letter was supportive and affirming during that challenging time.

Mickey Mantle

9-2-1962—Saturday A.M.

Dear Jay,

It was good to hear your voice last night. I know the drive was long and tedious, but I hope you enjoyed seeing the country. Much of living can be pleasant—if one is able to look at the process in the correct perspective. You have always done this admirably—and I'm sure you'll continue to.

The start of football season—and the first 10 days of practice are always tough no matter how well prepared you are mentally and physically. The self-control and ability to push yourself—to do your best when you don't feel much like it—is probably the greatest value you receive from playing the game. It will stand you in good stead all your life.

I know you have high ambitions. This is a totally necessary state of mind for excellence of performance. But you must not press or be impatient. Mickey Mantle is never sure just which time at bat he'll hit the home run—but he goes to the plate each time—set to do his best. This is the attitude you must strive to perfect. Do your total, all out best, on every single play. Never be discouraged if you don't do too well—or over elated when you make a good play. Simply do the best you have in you again on the next down.

It was wonderful having you home—and being here myself a bit more than usual these past few weeks. I hope next summer I can be available all of the time. My job in Washington is interesting—and I hope helpful to many young people, but I do hate being away from home as much as is necessary to be able to keep abreast of the situation.

Our squad looked in good shape at our meeting yesterday. We'll soon know. I hope we can play well—and see you in the Orange Bowl.

I'm truly proud of you, Jay, in all respects. Character, kindness and thoughtfulness toward other people, and an unselfish attitude of service to others are the qualities which make a man.

Love always,
Dad

While I was eager to begin the new football season, I was not as excited to begin the arduous task of fall workouts. It was also difficult to say goodbye to family and friends in Norman, but my life was made a little easier by the fact that I now had my own car. Freshmen were prohibited from bringing cars on campus at Duke. Not having a car in my sophomore year was a bit problematic, but on those occasions when I went out on a date, my fraternity brothers almost always came to my assistance. My new car was a 1962 Chevy Nova that I had purchased for $2,000 with money saved from working construction jobs and with the financial assistance of my parents.

If one were to drive from Norman to Durham today, the trip, covering about twelve hundred miles, would take approximately eighteen hours. In my college days it took much longer. The interstate highway system was still in its infancy; the four-lane highway was much more the exception than the rule. As Dad suggested in his letter, I did get a much closer look at the South while heading back to school, although I think his view on that sort of thing was more romantic than mine.

Patience is not always the strongest virtue of the young. I was no exception. As a young man, I occasionally found myself lost in thought, and too much time spent in self-focused thought can frequently lead to worry. Dad encouraged me to try to stay in the moment and not let anxiety about the future overwhelm me; to do that, though, required patience. One of the greatest lessons anyone can learn is to put failure behind as quickly as possible. That mindset is key in virtually every sport, from football to basketball, baseball to golf.

I was fortunate to have scored on a punt return the first time I touched the ball as a varsity player in college. Intellectually, I knew repeating that feat time and again would be impossible, yet emotionally, my goal every time my number was called was to break into the clear and go all the way. Mickey Mantle's aim every time he made a plate appearance for the New York Yankees may have been to hit a home run, and he hit 536 in his career, but he also struck out more than 1,700 times. A great sportsman like Mantle accepted failure as part of the equation to reach success. Yet he always set out to do his best every time at bat, regardless of the circumstances.

The other constant in Dad's formula for winning was preparation. Two-a-day practice sessions in the pre-season were indeed a challenge for players, but they also were an opportunity. Coaches understood that a player who overcame the rigors of morning and afternoon workouts was prepped to excel in the fourth quarter of a close game. Dad also believed that learning to do one's best when under great physical strain was not only the stuff of championship-caliber performance but was also a critical lesson away from the athletic arena. His advice strengthened my determination to fight through the exhausting times with a new perspective and to view the circumstances in a more positive light.

But perhaps the most important words of Dad's first letter to me at school in my junior year were contained in his last paragraph. While many might cite a football player, a "gridiron gladiator," as a classic example of manly demeanor, Dad offered a very different definition for what made a true man: "character, kindness and thoughtfulness toward other people, and an unselfish attitude of service to others" were what he expected of himself and those around him. They were also what he hoped for in me.

⋘⋙

Rugged Hills

9-11-1962—Monday

Dear Jay,

I hope your ball club is faring better with injuries than ours. Skidgel hurt an ankle before practice started. Mayhue is out because of a head injury and Sanderfeld sprained his ankle the 2nd day and will miss our first couple of games. In spite of all this, I felt yesterday we'd meet you in the Orange Bowl—mainly because Tommy Pannell is such a great player.

This morning in pass scrimmage, he broke his ankle and is out for the season. Jay, I can't really adequately express this boy's value to our team. True, we'll have him for three more years which will be great—but with him—this year—we'd have won. Sometimes you feel a little "snake-bit"—and this is one of those times. Our team's attitude is marvelous—and we're going to be good anyway—but to say "I'm shaken" is an understatement.

I rather expected you'd call last night—Please do this Sunday. I know you're hot, tired, and probably sick of football practice—but this discipline—this putting up with a totally tough unhappy situation, is one of the great lessons of the game which you'll appreciate more and more as time goes on. No matter how hard things get in the future, it'll never be worse. Life has some rugged hills for us all—and this training enables you to climb them "with a song in your heart."

We miss you—and I think of you each day. I pray for your happiness, growth, and development—and love you with all my heart and soul.

Always,
Dad

After two challenging and difficult seasons, Dad was determined that his 1962 team would regain the prominence and glory of his past Sooner squads. His letter revealed more emotion and disappointment than I ever remembered seeing in him. Tommy Pannell was an accomplished athlete who had been one of my teammates at Norman High School. He was my successor there and had all the skills to direct OU as its starting quarterback. Of all the positions in football, the most critical to a team's success, and thus the one in which an injury can have the most adverse impact on a team as a whole, is starting quarterback. Dad's starting quarterback was lost before the season had even started.

Looking back through the years, I believe that the values Dad expressed to me in his letters are as meaningful today as they ever were. Character and integrity are never out of season. But some things have changed, too. Today's game of football is much more wide open offensively, and players are bigger, stronger, and faster on both sides of the ball. Gone is the notion of a player playing on both sides of the football. Today's players are specialists.

Other major changes involve the health and well-being of players. In my day, invasive surgical procedures were considered a "last-ditch" measure, and a player's intake of fluids was severely restricted during intense and prolonged physical exertion. The rationale was that a small cup of water in the midst of hot and grueling practice was akin to offering aid and comfort. Coaches and trainers, and even team doctors, believed that exertion without fluids of any kind built determination and character. Today we know that lack of hydration puts an athlete's well-being in jeopardy. The old philosophy was really not a good idea at all. All who suffered through the agony of those less-informed times wish it had not taken so long for the medical community to speak up!

The 1962 football season would begin shortly. Duke's first game against the University of Southern California was one of the biggest games of our college careers. We were set to travel coast to coast with many experienced and seasoned players, including All Americans Art Gregory and Jean Berry and future All American Mike Curtis. Both teams were ranked among the nation's best, and a Blue Devil victory in the famed Los Angeles Memorial Coliseum could launch our team to one of its greatest seasons in history. As a team, the "song in our hearts" at Duke was of one accord: vanquishing the USC Trojans. Dad's next letter focused on that game and on OU's remarkable opening victory against Syracuse in Norman.

⋖⊰⋗⋘⊱⋗

The Vitally Important Factor

9-24-1962—Saturday Night

Dear Jay,

I was sorry about your game. I saw the last half. Your team moved the ball well. When in the 4th quarter you came back from 2nd and 30 to move to a first down on their 18, I was sure you'd carry it in—go for 2 points and win.

Speaking as an unbiased observer, I felt you were the best back on the field—both offensively and defensively.

This defeat can make your team. There's always a tendency to let down when you're broke, hurt. You have the talent on your squad—and losing shakes out overconfidence. If everyone plays with dedication—you'll win the rest.

We won today—and I almost feel guilty about it. Syracuse was better in every phase of the game except heart—courage, and the will to win. They kicked a field goal with 1:20 left in the first half to lead 3 to 0. They had two good scoring opportunities the second half—but we stopped them. We broke a play for 46 yards to finish down on their 18 with 5 minutes left—and then got a clipping penalty and two off-sides.

They drove to our 20 and had 4th and one—we stopped them—got the ball—and Looney made a great run to win for us.

All I can say about our team is that we try hard—are tough—and think we can win. At first glance, this isn't much in the way of assets or talent—but the human heart—unafraid and dedicated—can accomplish undreamed of things.

We need to become consistent in our running attack—and our passers must improve if we're going to beat good teams—but I feel we will get better as the season goes along.

I hope you and your squad will rally and fight back. It must have been terribly hot—and I know how hard it is to maintain consistent effort under those circumstances. The fact you made that great 4th quarter drive should give you all confidence.

The vitally important factor in competition, Jay, is not the result of a single game or even the season's record—it's what you learn through the experience which carries over into all the other things you do throughout life. Sacrifice of time and self in preparation—making a determined, all-out effort—and still falling short can strengthen a man beyond any other experience if one can learn to go forward again with even greater determination to get the best out of yourself in the most trying of circumstances. This I know you can and will do.

Pat seems to be adjusting well. I know it has been hard for him, but as he becomes more involved in school—the time will pass quickly and pleasantly.

I hope you're able to concentrate well on your studies: Being able to meet the total obligations of the day with a planned schedule is never easy—but again, I know you can and will.

I love you, Jay. No father can ever be more fortunate than I am in having a son like you.

All my love, always
Dad

PS: I hope the car is performing well. Maybe you'd better return the registration papers so I can keep them in my lock box.

Best of luck this week!

On the first day of autumn, 1962, Dad and I began our respective football seasons and the outcomes could not have been more different. While both the Sooners and the Blue Devils tallied a single touchdown in our openers, OU's defense made that score stand as Dad's team knocked off Syracuse 7–3. The triumph extended OU's winning ways from the season before and set the stage for what would be the last of Dad's fourteen conference championships.

The game also marked the debut of one of the most gifted athletes to play for Dad at Oklahoma. Joe Don Looney transferred from Cameron Junior College in Lawton, Oklahoma, and became Dad's first junior college transfer. Looney was in the vanguard of a new philosophy about the development and conditioning of an athlete's body. He weighed 220 pounds and was bigger, faster, and stronger than other OU players who carried the ball. I could feel Dad's adrenaline and excitement as he described Looney's sixty-yard scamper for the fourth-quarter touchdown that gave the Sooners their win against the Orangemen and gave Looney a spot among Dad's regulars.

As Duke opened its season on the West Coast, the nationally televised showdown against Southern California gave Dad a chance to see my teammates and me play, at least for the second half. What he saw was one of the bitterest defeats of my football career. We jumped out to an early lead as I caught a twenty-five-yard first-quarter scoring pass from Blue Devil quarterback Gil Garner. USC bounced back on two scoring passes in the second quarter, but from that point forward, five interceptions spelled our doom. Favored going into the game, Duke lost 14–7. USC would go on to an undefeated season and capture the school's fifth national championship in football.

To overcome adversity Dad taught that a player first must have the courage to compete by actually being in the arena. Second, he stressed the importance of overcoming misfortune by going forward again with even greater determination. It was in this way, he believed, one could get the best out of oneself in the most difficult of circumstances, an important lesson in all walks of life.

Despite the ecstasy and agony of our season-opening contests, Dad and I had to put those results behind us quickly. In week two of the season, Oklahoma would face Notre Dame while Duke would do battle with the University of South Carolina in our Atlantic Coast Conference opener.

⋘⋙

On Happiness

10/19/62—Thursday Night

Dear Jay,

I've been a poor correspondent lately. When one says they've been busy—in a sense it's true. But actually, with proper discipline plus the ability to make decisions—which I seem to lack lately—there should be time for all worthwhile things.

Pat enjoyed being at Duke last weekend, but said he was concerned about you. I am too, Jay. I know you're doing a good job in football and your studies—but I don't think you're "living happily." Many people go through their entire lives chasing a rainbow—are never happy with present circumstances, but in reflection—realize that days gone-by were great—even though they didn't realize it at the time because they were so busy chasing a rainbow of projected future—that they failed to realize that things weren't perfect—but were still good.

I'm probably not making the point well—but I feel sure, in spite of your loneliness and longing—your lack of confidence in your grades—your fatigue at football practice—that in retrospect—the fall will have been a time you truly "lived" because of the challenges involved—your adjustment and ability to meet them.

Abe Lincoln has been quoted on many aspects of human life—but my favorite of his quotes is: "People are about as happy as they make up their minds to be." This is an axiomatically true statement.

Each night after practice I'm sad and let down—We are a fine team except at QB and RH—but playing without a QB is like a car without a motor. Never have I had a team try as hard as we did at Texas— yet we lost. We can win the conference—but only by out-fighting our opponents. We lack skill and must make up for it with courage. Saturday is the big game. We'll do our best and I hope it will be good enough. In recognizing our shortcomings—which can't be rectified—and seeing our other men playing confidently and well—I'm more frustrated than I've ever been. But I'm still trying—and being as happy as I can.

I started out to give you a pep talk— and am winding up giving one to myself!!

I'll truly be pulling for you against Clemson. It is a thrill to start a game—even though we coaches say it doesn't make any difference. I know you'll play well.

Try hard to be happy, Jay, with the present while still looking forward to the future. I love you—and I'm more proud of you than words can express.

Always,
Dad

Dad's Sooners followed their win against Syracuse with back-to-back, although not unexpected, losses to Notre Dame 13–7 and Texas 9–6. Dad took encouragement from his team's performance in both games, but in the end OU made too many mistakes to triumph against the stiff opposition. Yet for Dad, the "second season" was at hand as OU prepared to open Big Eight conference play at Kansas against a Jayhawk team that had shut out the Sooners in Norman the year before.

My brother Pat, now enrolled at Johns Hopkins Medical School, attended Duke's 21–7 home victory over the University of California and sat with us on the sideline. Since Duke's opening loss against Southern California, we had defeated South Carolina and Florida, but the stress and pressure of academic studies continued to take a major toll on me. Relieved with our win over the Cal Bears and elated with Pat's visit, I made the mistake of partying a bit too much with my brother at a Phi Delt event that weekend. With my tongue loosened, I poured out my heart to Pat about the pressures I felt both academically and athletically. He later told Dad about our conversations.

I knew enough about American history to understand that if Abraham Lincoln could profess to the value of enjoying life, then it was not unreasonable to hope that I could do the same. For those intrinsically involved in the game of football, the sport can be an unforgiving taskmaster. If Lincoln could find personal happiness at a time when the nation over which he presided had split apart and fellow countrymen slaughtered one another on the battlefield, I should be able to put the worries of my own life in perspective. Easier said than done, but winning certainly helped achieve a more encouraging outlook.

While Duke won its fourth in a row, besting Clemson 16–0, the Sooners defeated Kansas in Lawrence 13–7. After Dad retired from coaching, he seldom displayed pictures on his office walls relating to his career as a head coach. One notable exception was the photograph of Monte Deere hugging him after that year's Kansas game. The triumph was significant in that it represented both resilience and determination. The victory at KU was but the first step toward a possible conference title.

And at the season's halfway point, the possibility still existed that Dad and I could share a common destiny in that season's Orange Bowl. A bid to the game would represent the attainment of goals we were both working hard to achieve. But then it occurred to me, like a sudden movement witnessed out of the corner of one's eye, how I would feel if placed in a spot where my success would mean my father's failure. Suddenly, I was not so sure that would be a good thing.

⟨⟩⟨⟩⟨⟩

Cuban Missile Crisis

10/25/1962—Thursday A.M.

Dear Jay,

It was good to talk with you last night. I share your concern over the international situation, but don't believe it is actually a bit different now than it has been for the past 8 or 10 years.

The so-called "cold war" is an actual war—in being—in every way except that there are no overt military operations: On the psychological, economic, and propaganda fronts we are at war and have been for some time: Military operations haven't begun because the Russians know they can't win. As long as we maintain our ability, in the literal sense, to absolutely blast Russia and every living thing there off the face of the earth, there will be no war.

For your generation it is a hard, long road of constant preparedness. In our Christian society we earnestly strive for peace and freedom—but recorded history shows that man—being men—in all ages and generations—has lived in war or the threat of war. It is not pleasant—but unfortunately, it has always been an unpleasant fact of life along with illness, hunger, privation, etc.

Mom said you told her football didn't seem too important now. Actually, Jay, it never has been as an end in itself. Although people distort the idea, the fact remains that the game is fundamentally educational for the participants. As Admiral Byrd said about exploring the Pole—"It isn't getting to the Pole that counts. It's what you learn on the way."

This is the best brief analysis of football. It isn't winning or losing that has lasting value or importance. The effort, the dedication, the sacrifice you make for a cause—your team—the working with others toward a common, most demanding goal. The loyalty, the joys, the disappointments, and above all learning to give your TOTAL best mentally, emotionally, and physically. These are qualities that make a man. And there is no other place they are learned so well.

You will find as you grow older that your football experience will have given you an inner strength and discipline which will enable you to meet the vicissitudes of life and fortune with your head high and your banners flying because you will know what hard, demanding preparation truly is—and that life's challenge is not actually from outside events—but rather with your own self—to do, always the very best of which you are capable.

When you do this—as you always do—you have literally won regardless of the score. I should add that it has been my experience that the score will be right too—(the personal or business situation included) because most people are incapable of delivering their best in all situations. MacArthur said: "On these fields of friendly strife are sown the seeds that on other fields in future years, will bear the fruits of victory." He didn't mean only war and battles. He was speaking of all human affairs.

I'm looking forward to seeing you soon—and I'm pulling for the Blue Devils. Good luck this week.

Love always,
Dad

On the evening of Monday, October 22, 1962, speaking to a nationwide television audience, President Kennedy addressed a "difficult and dangerous" series of events unfolding on the island of Cuba. He said: "We no longer live in a world where only the actual firing of weapons represents a sufficient challenge to a nation's security to constitute maximum peril. Nuclear weapons are so destructive and ballistic missiles are so swift, that any substantially increased possibility of their use or any sudden change in their deployment may well be regarded as a definite threat to peace." It was not difficult to imagine, based on the remarks of the president, that the country, and perhaps the entire world, was on the brink of nuclear war.

Like many other students at Duke, after watching the president's speech I called home. So many long-distance calls were being placed that it took me several tries before my call went through, adding to my anxiety over the news all of us had just learned.

Mom answered my call but told me Dad was not home from an after-practice meeting. While upset at the president's address, Mom remained calm and offered her reassurance. With so many others looking to reach loved ones at home, I was able to speak to her only briefly.

Not until the morning of October 28, thirteen days after ballistic missile sites were discovered in Cuba, did the premier of the Soviet Union, Nikita Khrushchev, announce to his countrymen that he had agreed to remove the weapons. The crisis had been averted. As Dad had suggested in his letter, the United States was able to negotiate successfully with its adversary from a position of strength. In the meantime, even with this ominous series of events hanging over the head of every American—and Soviet—man, woman, and child, both Duke and Oklahoma played football games, and both teams won.

This is one of my favorite letters from my father because he was able to take an international crisis and turn it into a teachable moment.

When he first became head coach at OU, he had two large signs installed in the locker room. When players headed out of the locker room door for practice or on game days, they passed under a sign that famously read: "Play like a Champion Today." Signs bearing the exact same words now hang in locker rooms throughout our country. Significantly, the sign says nothing about winning or the outcome of the game. It speaks to preparation and performance, giving one's best when it matters most.

For Dad the scoreboard was just one aspect of winning. When he wrote that "it isn't winning or losing that has lasting value or importance," he was not suggesting that the final outcome of a game was unimportant. His extraordinary record of on-field success gave testimony to the fact that winning mattered to him a great deal. His philosophy, however, was never about the outcome of any single game or life event. It was more about the journey to reach the final goal. Winning his way was about a process in which one's values, attitude, preparation, and perseverance, coupled with dedication to and sacrifice for a cause and for the good of one's own team, were what matter most. Success is a natural and inevitable extension of this process.

I later learned that the same holds true for almost any venture. In business, the scoreboard is represented by monthly, quarterly, and annual sales, revenue, and bottom-line goals and objectives. That is the way companies keep score. My father's definition of winning also means treating others—clients, co-workers, friends, neighbors, and especially fellow family members—with dignity and respect. He knew that for many, especially parents, winning sometimes was simply about getting home at a reasonable hour, making dinner, or reading to the kids at bedtime. For Dad, when individuals or teams dedicated themselves to preparing the right way, winning took care of itself.

Less well known was the sign my Dad had put up at the back of his team's locker room, best viewed when players first arrived. It was a literal reminder to each of his young men to "Be a Champion—Both on and off the Field." For Dad, that was what mattered most.

⋘⋙

Discipline of Disagreeing

November 12, 1962

Dear Jay,

I am sorry not to be writing personally, but things have been very busy and the last couple of weeks will remain so. I believe you can win the rest of them. 8 and 2 is a marvelous record. If we win Saturday I am a little sad that after such a fine season you may have to play against Oklahoma in the Orange Bowl!

Have been thinking a great deal about your problem as it relates to football practice, time, fatigue versus freshness, etc. You are probably already doing this, but the greatest training I know for any man is to be in some sort of disagreement with the procedures of his superiors and still be able to perform with total loyalty and devotion. The discipline of disagreeing in your own mind, and then still performing to the full limits of your ability is one of the great lessons all of us need to learn.

I thought you might enjoy the enclosed poem. Believe me, it is the truth.

I hope you can organize your time schedule so that you will get your term papers in. Actually, there are enough hours in the day if you don't waste any. Most of us do. If I were better organized I would have time to write this letter in long hand. I hope you can do a little better than I am doing.

Love always,
Dad

Since the Kansas victory, OU had posted wins over Kansas State, Colorado, and Iowa State. Duke defeated Clemson and North Carolina State but lost 20–9 to Georgia Tech in Durham, which in effect eliminated any possibility of an Oklahoma-Duke Orange Bowl matchup.

Coach Bill Murray was a superb football coach—his teams were well prepared and well disciplined. But during the season he never deviated from his practice schedule. Duke practiced in the tenth week of the season exactly as we had in the first week. We always had a two-and-a-half-hour practice with much running and physical contact. By mid-November I was exhausted, and the fatigue was not only impacting my ability to prepare for games but also having a negative impact in the classroom. I was irritated, and I had shared this with Dad, because I knew he shortened OU's practices to keep his players fresh as the season progressed.

Dad's advice was marvelous in its simplicity: Even when unhappy or in disagreement with one's circumstances, one still owes one's superiors total loyalty and devotion. In Dad's mind, it was a discipline issue. He expected me to perform to my utmost ability regardless of whether I saw eye-to-eye with my coaches. But rather than trying to put me in my place, he lifted me with his empathy and compassion. I believe this was one of his greatest strengths as both a father and a leader.

In the following weeks Oklahoma turned back its two main rivals for the conference crown, blanking Missouri 13–0 and dominating the defending league champion, Nebraska, 34–6. A season-ending win over Oklahoma State secured an 8–2 record and Dad's fourteenth conference championship. Going undefeated in Big Eight play was good enough to earn Oklahoma the trip to the Orange Bowl.

In the end, 8–2 did not punch the Blue Devils' ticket to Miami or New Orleans. Duke won the final two games of the year, trouncing Wake Forest 50–0 and then besting arch-rival North Carolina 16–14. Despite our fine season, with our loss to Georgia Tech we failed to receive a bid to either the Orange or the Sugar Bowl.

In the early 1960s there were just eleven bowl games, including the four major classics, the Orange, Sugar, Cotton, and Rose bowls. Arkansas and Ole Miss were tabbed to play the Sugar Bowl, and OU would play against Alabama in the Orange Bowl. That left the Blue Devils with a "consolation prize"—a Gator Bowl invitation to face Penn State. While we had won yet another ACC title and would have agreed enthusiastically to play in a New Year's

Day game in either the Orange or the Sugar Bowl, we were less interested in participating in any other game. That meant several more weeks going through Coach Murray's meat-grinder practice regimen. Fortunately Coach Murray put the team's post-season fate to a player vote, with no pressure from the coaches, and the outcome was nearly unanimous.

We decided that preparation for our upcoming final exams was a more worthwhile endeavor than preparing for Coach Rip Engle's Nittany Lions. We declined the Gator Bowl invitation and thus brought our season to an end. Meanwhile, a young coach would be helping Engle prepare his Penn State team to face Florida in post-season play. Thirty-six-year-old Joe Paterno was still three seasons removed from taking the reins as head coach of the Nittany Lions.

Deep down inside, I was relieved. As the season had progressed, I had grown less and less enthusiastic about a possible Oklahoma-Duke Orange Bowl matchup. I had no interest in working against my dad; it was one thing to kid about it—but I could not see myself competing against him and the tradition I admired, respected, and loved. I was happy for his successes that year and tired of worrying about football.

⋘⋙

Big Three

December 1962—Monday A.M.

Dear Jay,

It was good to talk with you last night even though the connection was so bad I could hardly hear you.

For the past week, I have been thinking about Christmas vacation.

We've had a good year, and I would be mighty pleased if it was over and we didn't have to play a bowl game. We simply aren't of Bowl caliber—next year we might be—and it seems too bad, after a much better season than anyone anticipated, to get waxed in a Bowl. I don't mean to imply we'll give up—we'll do our best—and come out of the chute at them—but if they're a solid team—they'll win—and if their passing is as good as it's supposed to be—it could be a one-sided game.

I want very much to have you come to the game—and hope you will decide to and also believe I understand your mixed emotions about the whole thing. First, not having Duke participating is a disappointment. Next, I know you'd still rather be playing for OU (even though educationally, all things considered, I hope you understand and believe you have done the wise thing in going to Duke). To be in Miami semi-around our team makes the two thoughts expressed above sort of constantly rub against each other—and the way to avoid this, obviously, would be not to go.

On the other hand, I'm sure you'd have a great time and that the vacation would do you a world of good physically and mentally. Miami is different. It is as tropical as Hawaii. The beach is white sand. The golf and entertainment are as good as Las Vegas. You would be staying at a different Hotel from our team (about a block away). I have a car for you and Pat. You could see as little or as much of Mom and me as you care to—and you never need to see or be around our team at any time. If you'd like to work out with us, you could be Namath, the Alabama QB in practice!! Since you're a better thrower than he is, it would be a big help!!! Joking aside, I know you would have a completely fun, relaxing, pleasant time which would do you a world of good. Whatever you decide to do will be fine with me—I really mean it—but do think it through carefully. The older I get, the more I realize that people really don't care what other people do. You can be as anonymous as you care to be while in Miami.

When we talked to Pat last night, he said you might come to Baltimore for the weekend. If you do, I'll see you.

I leave Tuesday night and will be at the Conference meeting in KC until Thursday. Then I go to NY to make a TV fitness show for the Army on Friday. We have a Fitness Staff meeting set for Monday in Washington. I'm to see the President on Monday. (It's high time I straightened him out on several items!) I hope to be home by Tuesday, but maybe I won't be done in Washington until late Tuesday and will go home on Wednesday.

I told Pat if his studies were up that he should come to NY on Saturday and that we could have dinner, or a show, watch the Giants play on Sunday—and then fly or train back to school Sunday night. Why don't you call him? If you can get away the "Big Three" will have Saturday afternoon, evening, and Sunday in the Big Town. We'd have a great time—if you're up enough in your studies to get away for a short period. Remember too, you can study on the plane or train.

I'm to call Pat Wednesday, and I will call you too. If it doesn't seem possible to get to NY, we'll plan to get together in Baltimore (if you can). Don't worry about expenses to NY. This is a time we should splurge a little—and Howard [Neumann] and I are in the process of selling another film series to the National Guard.

If things don't work out to see you this weekend, Christmas will be here soon. Think carefully about Miami—and remember—what Lincoln said—"People are about as happy as they make up their minds to be."

All of your life, in every circumstance, there will be elements you wish were different. But every situation can be enjoyable if approached with the correct mental attitude.

I'm proud of you—love you—and miss you—but will see you soon.

As always,
Dad

Dad's 1962 team achieved a remarkable comeback from two early losses and once again reigned supreme as conference champions. OU had returned to football glory and the team had done it with defense. Although Monte Deere proved to be an admirable replacement at quarterback, Dad and his coach staff had worked hard to instill a sound scheme on the defensive side of the ball. Those efforts paid remarkable dividends. In ten regular-season games that year, Oklahoma gave up a total of five touchdowns. In fact, the 48 points allowed during the 1962 regular season stands second on the school's all-time list. Only the 1938 Sooners allowed fewer—a total of just 12 points, paving the way to OU's first-ever bowl appearance.

During the weeks before the Orange Bowl, Dad's calendar was filled with conference meetings, television shows, physical fitness events, and a meeting with President Kennedy during which the president accepted his request to attend the Orange Bowl game. It was easy for me to accept Dad's invitation to observe OU's practice before the team's departure for the Orange Bowl and to be there with him and his team on the sidelines during the game in Miami. I knew many of the OU players and felt welcomed, although it remained somewhat awkward and emotional for me to be there and not be part of the team.

Before the game President Kennedy paid a visit to the Sooner locker room and offered the team a few comments. His words of encouragement did not inspire the squad. If anything, they may have proven a distraction. OU fumbled twice inside the 10-yard line, and unfortunately, as Dad had predicted, the Sooners lost the game 17–0 to an outstanding Alabama team led by quarterback Joe Namath, linebacker Lee Roy Jordan, and the team's indomitable coach, Paul "Bear" Bryant.

After the game, Bryant came to Dad's hotel suite to visit with him and a small group of my father's friends and family. Coach

Bryant was a football legend who won more than three hundred games in his coaching career. He was head coach at the University of Kentucky when his team broke OU's thirty-one-game winning streak at the Sugar Bowl on January 1, 1951.

He and Dad had remained close friends throughout their careers and, following that Sugar Bowl game, had agreed to meet each year during a weekend in the spring at a hotel somewhere in the South or Southwest to discuss football. Their meetings rotated between Memphis, Dallas, and several other cities. Their suites included a large living room and adjoining bedrooms and always featured a blackboard to enable them to partake in "chalk talk" as they explained to each other what they had learned about football in the preceding twelve months. Both men were adamant throughout their hall-of-fame careers that they never stopped learning when it came to football—or, in my dad's case, virtually anything else. Football junkies, sportswriters, or coaches would have given anything to have been a fly on the wall to hear those historic discussions.

Coach Bryant's cordial company made Oklahoma's defeat a little more bearable, if you'll pardon the pun. I had met Bryant several times before and felt comfortable chatting with him. "Coach," I said, "I believe if OU had not fumbled twice inside your 10-yard line, we would have won the game." He looked me straight in the eyes and responded in his slow, deep, southern drawl, "No, Jay. Even if OU had scored both touchdowns, I still believe we're going to find a way to win!" He said it with such conviction and intensity that he made a believer out of me. It was not until years later that I realized this was the unique nature of Bryant's brand of leadership. Needless to say, I enjoyed the evening in the company of two of college football's all-time greatest coaches.

Up the eastern seaboard, another event took place on that same day, January 1, 1963, which would have a major impact on my father's life. The powerful and legendary Oklahoma politician Robert S. Kerr died in Washington, D.C., where he served his state and his nation as a member of the U.S. Senate. The day after the Orange Bowl, Dad held a somewhat clandestine meeting with Oklahoma governor J. Howard Edmondson to discuss filling Kerr's vacant seat. Dad suggested that Edmondson resign as governor and have his successor, the current lieutenant governor, George Nigh, appoint him as Kerr's replacement until an election could be held to fill out Kerr's term. Edmondson chose to follow Dad's advice to the letter, and within just a few days, Oklahoma had both a new governor and a new United States senator without a single vote being cast.

At this time Dad had not made a decision to pursue a career in politics, but as a result of those discussions, I learned for the first time that he might be interested in considering that possibility at a later date.

❦

The Broyles Way

2/24/1963—Sunday

Dear Jay,

These have been mighty busy weeks. Four weekends ago we were in Pittsburgh and Boston—then the next weekend Grand Rapids and St. Louis—last week, Dallas and Houston—this week Los Angeles and San Francisco. Next weekend it will be Atlanta and Washington. Then, thank goodness, the clinics will be over.

In between, I've been gone almost every night recruiting. I will need to stay over in Washington for a couple of days next week and then go to NY before getting home for a while.

The clinics have been very successful—with one or two exceptions. In another year, we should make quite a bit of money on them and at the same time provide a real service for the coaches.

Our recruiting has been fairly successful. We're going to meet tomorrow to see exactly where we stand and will then try to decide what to do to fill out our squad. Except for Arkansas we've competed quite well. Apparently, Broyles tells everyone he'll be All American—that school will be easy, etc.—which I simply cannot do. It seems to be effective with poor students though.

How is spring practice? I'll be anxious to know if you're playing—and what position. I felt you had a fine team last year—and join in your hope that you'll be truly great this season.

We begin our spring practice on March 12. I'm most anxious to see the freshmen. If we can find four or five good linemen in the group and a couple of fast backs—we could be a pretty good team. We'd better be if we hope to stay on the field with Southern California.

I'll be flying from Atlanta to Washington next Saturday night. Pat is going to meet me and spend the weekend with me. If you aren't involved in too much studying, football, or social life, why don't you fly up Saturday night and join us. Think it over, and call Pat to let him know if you can do it.

It seems like a long time since I've seen you. It will be great to be together again—either next weekend or for Easter vacation. I hope your ulcer is healed and that you're feeling well.

> All my love, always
> Dad

On the heels of his Sooners' return to glory, Dad was once again in the middle of college football's second most important season: recruiting. Being consistently competitive requires having players with equal or superior athletic talent as compared to the opposition. Given OU's outstanding tradition, established before his arrival at the school and then bolstered considerably by his success, Dad always felt he had a competitive advantage when it came to recruiting top players.

As the recruiting wars were being waged, Dad was having particular difficulty coming to terms with the approach of his friendly rival from Fayetteville, Arkansas: Frank Broyles. Dad maintained a high regard for Broyles, whom he considered a good friend and an outstanding coach, but he was irritated about some Arkansas recruiting successes that would soon take the school to its first-ever national championship in 1964 and a twenty-two-game winning streak. Some of Dad's frustration had to do with losing top talent to the Razorbacks, but he was mainly irked by some of the promises he learned Arkansas coaches were making to prospects. Dad believed in being honest with recruits as well as their parents.

Meanwhile, I had encountered a personal challenge of my own. Returning to Duke after the Orange Bowl and Christmas holidays, I began suffering acute stomach pains. When the problem persisted, my roommate Jim Miles insisted that I check myself into Duke Medical Center, where I was diagnosed with bleeding ulcers.

The stress of final examinations on top of the rigors of a demanding football season had finally got the best of me. My French studies remained a thorn in my side. At Duke, three years of coursework in a foreign language were a required part of the curriculum. I chose French and found myself reading fifteen to twenty pages of French novels each evening. Not only did I have to look up forty to fifty words for translation during each assignment, but I discovered, to my great dismay, I did not know the meaning of half the words in English! From my freshman to junior years, my French grade deteriorated from a B to a C and then to a D—the only time in my life my classroom marks fell below the C level. I remained in the hospital for ten days under the care of Dr. Julian Ruffin and eventually recovered.

The only positive aspect of the crisis was that after voting with my teammates to decline the Gator Bowl bid to avoid another month of Coach Murray's practice gauntlet, thanks to my ulcer I missed all of spring practice in my junior year, too.

⊰⊱

Definable Goals

4/25/1963—Thursday A.M.

Dear Jay,

Life is truly strange. When I accepted the speaking engagement in Charlotte four months ago, I did so only so I could visit and spend a couple of days with you. Now, here I am flying to Washington—and I'm not going to see you at all. I'm sorry that I won't, but trust you understand.

Mother and I were so pleased about your trip to Boston. Now that you know what your educational objectives will be, all of your studying should be easier because there will be a sense of direction; purpose, and a definable goal to your efforts.

When do you plan to visit the Seminary in Alexandria? It too is supposed to be fine in all respects. I think it would be prudent to visit— just as it was when you were deciding on Duke.

For selfish reasons, I would not be honest if I didn't tell you I hope you'll work in Norman this summer. I won't need to be gone much, and we could spend quite a bit of time together. As your responsibilities and obligations multiply, this will be increasingly difficult to do.

I expect to come East again in a couple of weeks. I'll call, and will hope we can get together for a day or two. I love you and am so proud of you.

Always,
Dad

PS: Take care of your ulcer! No worries!

On a windy spring day I landed in Boston on an Eastern Airlines turbo prop to visit the Episcopal Theological School, known as ETS, in Cambridge, Massachusetts. I was considering the possibility of pursuing a graduate degree in theology. My Duke major was in political science with a minor in religion, and I continued to have a deep interest in gaining a better depth and understanding of my faith to enable me to contribute to people in some significant way after graduation. During that trip my conversations with the dean and members of the faculty reminded me of my recruiting visit to Duke three years earlier. The big difference, of course, was that football was not a factor. In fact, with the NFL draft looming following my final year of eligibility at Duke, I was seriously considering taking my life in a completely new direction.

As at Duke, I felt comfortable with the surroundings and felt a connection with those I met. I found openness and honesty at ETS and I appreciated the school's focus on the spiritual nature of the secular world. Dad suggested I also take time to visit the Episcopal Theological Seminary in Alexandria, Virginia. But just as I was certain that Duke was the right choice for me after visiting Durham for the first time, I was content that if I chose to attend seminary school, ETS was where I wanted to be.

The Kind Thing to Do

5/15/63—Tuesday Night

Dear Jay,

It was good to talk with you Saturday, but it will be even better to have you home. We had a letter from Pat today. He said he'd enjoyed the weekend and that you seemed to be looking and feeling better than you had for a long time. I hope your ulcer is totally healed and that you have no more trouble with it.

Ethel was released from the hospital on Sunday so Mother flew to Naples to spend a few days with her. Ethel needed her badly—and while I know Mom would much prefer to be here—it was the considerate, kind thing to do. Ethel will enjoy having her—and I expect the two ladies will catch up on much gossip.

Our Conference spring meeting begins in Manhattan, Kansas on Thursday. We don't have much on the Agenda, so it should be a quick session. Thursday afternoon, we have a golf tournament. My game has been terrible, but I'm going to rally up and wear the red and white with pride and distinction.

Mother is going to fly from Minneapolis to Washington on Sunday, and I'll fly from here. We hope to have dinner with Pat Monday night—and wish you, too, could be with us.

It won't be long until you're home. It will be so good to see you. There are so many things I hope to discuss with you.

I love you and miss you, but look forward to seeing you soon.

Always,
Dad

I was nearing completion of the second semester of my junior year at Duke and was anxious to return home for the summer. My ulcer had healed, and I was looking forward to a change of pace. In late July my parents drove me to the Mayo Clinic in Rochester, Minnesota, for a routine checkup.

In 1951 Dad had had emergency surgery at the Mayo Clinic for a bowel obstruction, and during that procedure, doctors discovered a testicular lump. A biopsy revealed cancer and the testicle was removed. Dad always felt fortunate and grateful his cancer was detected early.

As a result of his own health scare, Dad became a regular at the Mayo Clinic, returning each year for a complete physical. He trusted the doctors there and encouraged me to get myself checked out to ensure that my ulcer was fully healed. During the examinations I was shocked when X-rays revealed a new and even larger ulcer in my duodenum. Once again I was hospitalized immediately. I remained in Rochester, about three and a half hours from Mom's hometown of Grinnell, Iowa, for ten days of convalescence. Alone in my hospital bed and just a month before my final season at Duke, I began to have serious doubts about the possibility of playing in my senior year. With my future in the game jeopardized, I realized just how fortunate I had been to play the game at such a high level. My reflection helped to put things into the right perspective.

When I returned to Duke for my senior season my physician there, Dr. Ruffin, determined that my condition would probably be worsened if I sat on the sidelines chewing my fingernails. He thought there would actually be less stress in playing, so he approved my return to the team. One advantage of being hospitalized was that I had lost ten pounds and as a result was much faster. As a senior, I was alternate captain with Chuck Walker, an all-ACC tackle who later enjoyed a twelve-year NFL career with the St. Louis Cardinals.

Before I returned to Duke, Dad continued to emphasize the importance of helping others, focusing on my teammates instead of just me. Our season began with three straight victories over South Carolina, Virginia, Maryland and a 20–20 tie with California at Berkeley, followed by a victory over Clemson. I played well in the 35–30 victory over Clemson, scoring touchdowns on a thirty-eight-yard pass reception and a sixty-seven-yard run. For my performance, I was named AP National Back of the Week.

As if trying to show how that never-realized Oklahoma-Duke Orange Bowl might have turned out, OU opened its season against Clemson and knocked off the Tigers 31–14. The next week, a year after Duke's unsuccessful visit to the LA Coliseum, OU traveled to the City of Angels and, on an afternoon that featured record-breaking temperatures above 100 degrees, the Sooners defeated the defending national-champion Trojans 17–12. OU then lost for the sixth year in a row to Texas before an important win of 18–15 against the Gale Sayers–led Kansas Jayhawks who opened conference play, setting the stage for Dad's final letter to me at Duke.

When he learned of Duke's first season loss, he offered the following consolation.

Lose Yourself in Others

October, 1963

Dear Jay,

It was so good to talk to you last night. When I heard the score, I knew how disappointed you'd be. You must realize that times have changed in football, and if you have a schedule with comparable teams, you just are not going to win them all. Southern California is a good example. I'm sure they're the best in the country—yet they've already been defeated twice. In 60 minutes anything can happen—and usually does.

The only thing that concerns me about your situation is your continued deep concern with yourself and your attitude. All of us must be analytical and honest with ourselves if we are going to learn and profit from our mistakes and be better men in the future. But you can do this so much of the time that it becomes damaging, not a helpful thing.

You need to prepare yourself mentally and physically for everything that you do. When the task is over—a game, an examination, a speech, an interview, a business presentation, anything—you must analyze your performance and make notes of what you could have done better. Resolve to do those things better—through attention to detail and practice—and then go on to the next of life's tests and problems.

The greatest of all things you can do to clarify, help, and improve your own attitude from being too self-centered is to do what I have said above—and then *literally lose yourself in helping others with their concerns and problems.*

When Christ said, "you must lose yourself to find yourself," he was not speaking of material things—fasting, giving away all worldly goods, not caring about your appearance or abilities. On the contrary, he meant be as good, as capable as you can be; then use that talent for the benefit of others—to help others.

If you are not a talented, producing, capable man, you can't really do much for others. But with a degree of wisdom and great compassion, you can turn outward in love to help others. Every man, deep in his soul has ambition. Those who appear not to, are frustrated—perhaps by laziness—or lack of talent—but most often by lack of understanding attitudes from others which drives them into their self-protective shells.

Your honest concern for others, while trying to be honest with yourself, but not worrying about yourself beyond recognizing where, why, and how you can improve, is a real secret to a joyous, contributing life. "Lose yourself to find yourself." In your association with any organization your attitude is the key. "What can I get out of it"—what the group can do for me—as opposed to "what can I contribute" to the success of the group.

You always have done those things, Jay, which is why you are such a wonderful person. I mention them only to help you reaffirm your own faith, belief, and understanding—not because I have even the slightest concern that you haven't already lived and practiced these precepts.

We had a remarkably fine sermon at early communion this morning by the SMU Episcopal chaplain who was visiting. He pointed out that science has advanced so rapidly it has shattered our previous understanding of the world . . . What we knew and thought about the world a century or even 50 years ago was vastly different from what we know to be true today.

In this shattering of these beliefs, many of us have made the fatal mistake of feeling there is nothing in which we can believe. But the guiding moral precepts and faiths which are the foundation of our society are still eternal in the best sense of the word.

Our increased knowledge of the nature of God's world in no way alters the truth of these precepts.

He then pointed out that being human in spite of our profound wishes—we were hypocrites in the sense we were unable to live up to our ideals. But he added, this was the great gift of Christ. The honest effort, the falling short, the forgiveness, and once again the effort. This is applicable to all living, particularly football.

I've probably gone on longer that I probably should, but all I've said is so full in my heart, I wanted to share it with you. I love you deeply and I'm so proud of the man you've become.

All my love always,
Dad

Only one letter from my father survives from my final year as an undergraduate student at Duke. I know he wrote to me just as frequently as during my sophomore and junior years, but disappointingly, some of Dad's letters have simply vanished.

Duke lost to North Carolina State 21–7 in Raleigh for the season's first loss after getting off to a great start with a record of 4–0–1. Dad conveyed an understanding of emotions associated with defeat and did his best to assuage my feelings. Sometimes people lose focus when events do not unfold as planned. He captured the essence of my giving back to others—whether to individuals or groups or teammates. Giving to others was an important part of his philosophy, and it applies during good times and bad.

My senior year at Duke was a time of many injuries as the season progressed. We dropped games against Georgia Tech and a gifted Navy team led by Roger Staubach, and then had a win against Wake Forest. We were prepared to play North Carolina in Durham for our final game. A victory would mean a tie for the ACC Conference championship and a fourth consecutive conference title.

On the Friday afternoon before our North Carolina game, I awakened from a nap before practice to learn of President Kennedy's assassination. Like almost all other games, the Duke–North Carolina game was postponed. Since Dad was one of the few coaches who personally knew the Kennedys well, he called the president's executive assistant Ted Reardon to ascertain the Kennedy family's direction. Robert Kennedy's advice was to play the games as scheduled.

Few universities followed that advice, but based on Dad's conversation, OU played Nebraska in Lincoln and lost 29–20. Many OU players later conveyed how difficult it was to play as a visitor on a cold gray day during such a time of national grief. Rick McCurdy, a great OU all-conference end, observed: "I think we should not have played the game. I think we were all ready to go back home. Had we been in Oklahoma with our own family and our own friends, we would have been the victors. If they had been the visiting team I think they would have lost just because of the situation."

The next week OU defeated Oklahoma State 34–10 in Norman to complete the season with a respectable 8–2 record. The same day Duke lost to North Carolina 16–14 on a forty-seven-yard field goal in the final seconds of the game for a 5–4–1 record. Had we held on, we would have been co-ACC champions.

That football season was my best ever—Atlantic Coast Conference Player of the Year; first team on the American Football Coaches All American Team; the UPI All American Team and *Look* All American Team; and eighth in the Heisman Trophy balloting, won that year by Navy quarterback Roger Staubach. I participated in the East-West Shrine Game, the Hula Bowl, and the American Football Coaches All Star games, which gave me an opportunity to play with and against future NFL stars like Paul Warfield, Charlie Taylor, and Carl Eller.

Reflecting on my career at Duke, I realize how fortunate I was to have had a father and friend who took the time to write and to help me adjust to a challenging period of growth. Dad's consistent encouragement, support and love built my confidence and strengthened my resolve when I was emotionally down and distressed, helping me understand how both football and academics would prepare me for the future.

PART IV

Graduate School Years

1964–1966

> The power of a movement lies in the fact that it can
> indeed change the habits of people. This change is not
> the result of force but of dedication, or moral persuasion.
>
> Stephen Biko, South African anti-apartheid
> activist

Ironically, Dad and I gave up football at the same time and in many respects were in the process of reinventing ourselves simultaneously. I had played the game competitively since being a fourth grader at McKinley grade school in Norman. He had been at it much longer, beginning informally with the 50th Street Tigers in Minneapolis, who included the great women's golf legend Patty Berg, a resident in the same neighborhood. He remained formally connected to football from grade school until he left OU. The handwritten response in the spot for "father's occupation" on my birth certificate (April 11, 1942) was "football coach." From the time Pat and I were born, Dad was already in the coaching profession.

He resigned his head coach and athletic director positions at OU in December 1963 and announced his candidacy for the United States Senate in February 1964. I decided to forgo an NFL experience, as a probable first round draft pick, to enter graduate school at the Episcopal Theological School (ETS) in Cambridge, Massachusetts, a seminary affiliated with Harvard.

Many of my close friends' families in Norman, including the Lawtons, were members of St. John's Episcopal Church, which was a major influence during my teenage years. I liked Duke's religious atmosphere and enjoyed my role in its Fellowship of Christian Athletes chapter. Like many students in college, I went through a period of questioning my religious faith. As I took more religion courses at Duke, I became more interested in the Judeo-Christian tradition and religion.

Gradually, I regained my faith and was especially committed to helping the disadvantaged through general social and government work. Growing up in Oklahoma, I knew that public schools were generally segregated, but I never remember seeing segregated bathrooms or other segregated businesses or facilities. At Duke for the first time in my life I witnessed sit-ins, and although not an active participant, I was emotionally moved by the experiences. While I felt a spiritual calling to attend seminary, I was not certain it would lead to a role in the institutional church as a deacon or priest or in some other capacity. Either way I remained focused on the importance of Christian social ethics in our country and abroad.

I felt confident that I could play in the NFL, though the financial rewards were not close to what they are today, nor was the intense publicity. In discussions with teams I asked them not to waste a draft pick on me. I was selected anyway by the Kansas City Chiefs and Chicago Bears in later rounds, but playing professional football was not a priority for me because I did not have a yearning to prove myself on the football field. My desire to be of service to others and move ahead with my life dominated my thinking.

During my brother Pat's wedding in Dallas in the summer of 1963, I met Betty Dixon, a former Miss OU and Miss Oklahoma City and a bridesmaid in the wedding. We dated in Norman for the remainder of the summer before I returned for my final football season at Duke. We were married in January 1964 during my last semester.

Betty continued her interest in piano and graduated from Boston University in 1965 with a degree in music. Mom and Dad both adored her; his letters to us while I was in theological school reflect love and tenderness similar to his feelings for me. Our first daughter, Kirsten, arrived at Boston Lying-In Hospital during my second year at ETS. Our second daughter, Holly, was delivered fourteen months later in Oklahoma City after my graduation from ETS. (Betty and I were divorced ten years later but remain friends today.)

Dad had always been interested in national politics. Working in Washington, D.C., during the Kennedy Administration enabled him to observe for the first time the legislative process in our nation's capital and heightened his interest in running for public office. He was concerned that personal responsibility, initiative, and self-reliance could not flourish with centralization of power in Washington at the expense of cities, counties, and states. His final motivation came as a result of the Kennedy assassination. Despite his disagreement with many Kennedy Administration policies, Dad genuinely liked the president and his brother Robert. It was easy for him to schedule appointments on short notice because of the mutual respect they held for one another. The president's untimely death was an influential event for Dad—as for most Americans.

His campaign for the U.S. Senate in 1964 was the center of attention the entire summer. As it turned out, he was not running against Governor Edmondson after all. Oklahoma state senator Fred R. Harris had defeated Edmondson in a special election in 1964, and Dad's opponent was the state senator. Pat and I worked diligently on the campaign trail, going door to door on Dad's behalf. I left ETS during my first semester to return to Oklahoma to help for the final ten days of the campaign.

Unfortunately, Dad picked a bad year to run. Following the

assassination, the nation was looking for stability. A Lyndon Johnson landslide over Barry Goldwater would mean that Dad would have to pick up swing votes—people who might vote for Johnson for president as a Democrat and then switch to him as a Republican for the Senate vote. It did not happen. He lost the race by fewer than 22,000 votes when Johnson carried the state.

The death of his mother and his loss in the Senate race were the two biggest disappointments in his life. He was stung by the election results—going to bed the night before the election knowing the race would be close but believing he would ultimately win. And he lost. His father had taught him to look ahead during difficult times, not backward. He actively moved on with his life, knowing there would be other avenues for him to make significant contributions to society. Since he did not consider himself independently wealthy—and knowing that he would constantly be on the money-raising trail—political office was no longer an option for him.

Had Dad won the Senate race, I think he would have been a true statesman, just as he had been a great football coach. He had all the necessary qualities to perform that role exceedingly well. Spiro Agnew was a surprise nominee for vice president in 1968. I was at the Republican Convention in Miami Beach and remember the spontaneous disbelief from almost every journalist in the ballroom at the moment of Nixon's announcement at his press conference. Had Dad won, candidate Nixon might have selected his friend Bud Wilkinson to join him on the 1968 ticket. Who knows?

Returning to ETS for the completion of my first year was bittersweet with the emotional let-down of Dad's election loss. But I knew he would rebound quickly, and I was anxious to resume my graduate studies and get on with my life.

New Beginnings

2/11/1965—Thursday

Dear Jay and Betty,

Now that things are beginning to settle down I intend to be a much better correspondent. Since the election I seem to have been disorganized. I'm trying to resolve my own immediate future employment plans—and arrange firm contacts—and I have traveled more than I like to do—and have left far too many things undone.

Last Thursday night in New York we signed all of the Foundation papers. I have a three-year contract which in all its details is extremely favorable. On Friday, we had a press announcement luncheon which came off well.

While in New York I talked again with NBC about a TV contract. We are in agreement about the big terms, but are having trouble resolving the details related to my being exclusive for NBC and my political activities. We will get it all cleared up in a few days. As part of the contract, I will do the Pre-game NCAA game of the week show and some "color" work. I also am to be available for a limited number of appearances at other shows.

As Mom has told you, we have sub-let a small apartment in Washington. The address is 2500 Q St. NW. We have also leased office space for the Foundation at 1725 K St. NW. I'm on my way to Los Angeles now for our Clinics and will fly to Washington Sunday. I will be there next week and then do the Atlanta-Washington clinics next weekend. I'm going back to Oklahoma for the Republican Convention on February 27 and will drive to Washington with Mother as soon as the Convention ends. Mother is in Grinnell now and will visit Grandmother for about a week.

It will be fun to be in the East this spring. When you have time, let us know your spring vacation plans. Perhaps we can all get together at some fun spot for a few days.

Life's eternal problems remain mystifying to me. I know you are gaining a depth of insight. I look forward to talking with you leisurely about these most important factors of value. Our judgments as to what truly is important determine virtually all of our choices and the conduct of our lives.

I am candid enough to recognize that I have, hopefully, another 25 years in which to contribute to the world in what ways I can. What is the best course of conduct for me?

The political frontier remains challenging. You will be interested in reading the February 15 issue of *U.S. News and World Report*. There is an article about "Had Lincoln Lived Today" which clearly shows that the effort of the individual is the priceless ingredient in the development of character which leads to success and salvation. How the State [Government] can take over more and more personal and family responsibilities and still not suffocate and enervate the individual's self-reliance and responsibility remains the dilemma of our time. Our system is based on the independence and quality of the individual. We believe he will make careful valid judgments. How can he if he lacks self-reliance and initiative? Will he not vote for those who sound the siren's call to ease and avoidance of the responsibility of sacrifice in a worthy cause?

I know you are aware of all these problems and many more. It will be a joy to talk them over with you.

At times, while writing, the flight has been a bit rough. I hope you can read this without too much trouble.

I love you both, and am so proud of you.

Always,
Dad

The Episcopal Theological School is not far from Wellesley College and is off Harvard Square. I had never spent any time in New England. People's accents were noticeably different, the sun set much earlier in the fall and winter, and women's hairstyles and dress codes were much more informal. ETS had a distinguished faculty with renowned scholars, theologians, and authors including Harvey Guthrie and Joseph Fletcher. Its dean, John Coburn, continued to be a leader in the church for many years, teaching what is essential and important in the ministry and a life of faith.

Course work resembled what I had experienced at Duke, as it focused on similar academic fundamentals with the same class requirements. But there was a noticeable difference. ETS also exposed seminary students to the guts of life and death situations to be encountered later as priests or laymen of the church. It was not simply learning in the classroom. On Sundays seminary students spent the day working in a church or social organization, interacting with people. During summers they worked in hospitals, prisons, classrooms, or the inner city. While the focus was on a career as a deacon and then priest of the Episcopal Church, the ETS experience reached beyond the classroom and placed much emphasis on human experiences lived in the world. It meant not being withdrawn but being involved in both the joys and heartaches of life's situations.

My entering class was much smaller than at Duke—thirty-three students who had graduated from diverse colleges and universities around the country. There were required courses at ETS on the Old Testament, New Testament, and church history. As a student progressed there were optional courses in disciplines such as Christian social ethics or comparative world religions. At the completion of three years of study, one received a bachelor of divinity degree that today is the equivalent of a master's of divinity.

Coming off his loss in the U.S. Senate race, Dad contemplated his future contributions now that he was not to become a national public leader. From a moral perspective, his assumptions on political, theological, and athletic issues were the same. He knew what it took to build championship teams. A coach needed discipline and respect. He needed to be organized and to care for the well-being of those he taught. A player had to have a dedicated, determined, unselfish outlook and be willing to work tirelessly with others for an important cause. And Dad knew that when players did not make consistent efforts to be the best, they would not achieve championship status.

Those thoughts dominated his thinking in government and social policy and were the fundamental reasons he was motivated to seek elected office in the first place. When the federal government moved to take over more personal and family responsibilities, he feared that many people would choose to "take the easy way out." He thought a person, group, or nation could not build greatness—could not be its best—when responsibility, initiative, and self-reliance were eroded.

Dad was a pragmatist and had far more confidence in solid public and private partnerships to address social issues than in programs developed and mandated from Washington. He believed city, county, and state partnerships with private and civic organizations, in concert with federal input, could create better solutions.

Religion provided clues to solutions about how to assist disadvantaged, indigent, and underprivileged people of the world and at the same time to achieve excellence on an individual, group, or national level. But it was one thing to gain an understanding of Christian ethics, and quite another to face the problem of finding a direction from Christian ethics to social policy.

In most respects, the teachings of Jesus in the New Testament are couched in terms of one-to-one relationships. More complex and difficult ethical problems deal with questions about multiple people's responsibility to a single person or many people's responsibility to multiple people. In our discussions about a decision-making process to help others, my father always favored providing an opportunity for people who were being helped to retain initiative, responsibility, and self-reliance in the solution process. Without that critical factor, something important was missing for him.

⋙⋘

Preciseness of Vocabulary

2/20/1965—Saturday

Dear Jay and Betty,

Thank you so much for your letter. I'm pleased you are enjoying school. I know the experience is one of growth for you in a total way—in every sense—and that as such it is a most worthwhile experience.

One other factor you both recognize, I know, is that the joy of living is in doing. This is among the most misunderstood facts of our time. Most people because of propaganda and advertising by entities such as unions and insurance companies, etc.—seem to think the purpose of life is as little work—and as early a retirement as possible. Nothing could be farther from the truth. Happiness is in doing—in accepting, meeting, and conquering the challenges of life—and where possible in doing for others—not for yourself.

Your observation, Jay, that communication is the difficult problem of human understanding is clearly accurate. Unfortunately, the language barrier has been a prime cause of distrust which has led to war and strife of every kind. It is even a hard barrier to overcome among people who speak the same language.

I hold to the theory that pure science has outdistanced other intellectual fields during our time chiefly because of the preciseness of their vocabulary. The formulas and terms are in the exact center of the bull's eye to students regardless of their own native tongue. Such preciseness is totally unknown in the social studies, religion, and other fields. I became acutely aware of this as a coach. Football terminology is about as inaccurate as one can imagine. The same words mean a different thing to people on different teams!

I'm delighted you plan to do your paper on the Atonement. This is a concept I've never understood. I would imagine one of your chief problems is a complete and fearless break with the "sacredness" of concepts and ideas. I know you have the intellectual honesty and courage, however, to speak the truth your heart and mind tells you—regardless of the storm such actions may create.

Any break with the comfort of tradition is seldom popular—yet it is the only way we reach nearer to God. The search for God, I believe, is the search for truth because God is the truth.

Luther was the product of an honest conscience fortunately alive at the proper moment of political upheaval against the political influence of the church.

Most of history's great men were not admired, liked, or even accepted by their contemporaries. Begin with Socrates, Caesar, Galileo, Lincoln—and on down the line. The fact that popularity is the most emphasized of qualities—and therefore the least important—is immediately apparent.

I'm quite sure we can spend a week or more in some secluded spot during your vacation. Will work on it and get the dates sometime soon by phone so I can keep my schedule clear.

Betty, as soon as you know your recital date, let me know so I can keep the time free. Mary and I want to be there!!

I love you both—and so proud of you both—and will hope to see you soon.

Always,
Dad

I was beginning to learn how difficult communication is for people—especially the language used to convey religious truths—and I began to believe that it was perhaps humanity's most challenging problem. Dad's encouragement to maintain an intellectual honesty in my studies reminded me of his grandmother's advice to him as a young man—"dare to be a Daniel."

His belief that science had outdistanced other intellectual fields in communication chiefly because of the precision of its vocabulary was of great interest to me. Dr. Bill Carmack, former chair of the OU communications department, thinks Dad must have been aware of Alfred Korzybski, a Polish count, who fathered the field in the philosophy of languages called general semantics, taught by many colleges and universities and based on the assumption that scientific discourse is superior to ordinary language.

I also thought Dad's comparison of science to football terminology was profound. It is strange, but true, that in football the same words have diverse meanings to people on different teams; some defenses with players in identical positions and some passing and running plays and actual offensive formations have the exact same design but are called by different names. In the 1950s, as some of his coaching staff advanced to positions at other schools, including Pete Elliott, Eddie Crowder, and J. D. Roberts, Dad had a natural turnover of assistant coaches, some of whom used a vocabulary from coaching environments foreign to him. This necessitated meetings with his coaching staff to clarify the precise vocabulary and words for instruction that he expected.

His belief that all great leaders will ultimately be judged through history—not in the present—was a good reminder to me about the importance of integrity and honesty. Secular society's preoccupation with immediate popularity never mattered to Dad as a leader. What mattered to him was to be active and to be involved—everywhere possible, whether in graduate school, the police force, as a teacher, or in any profession.

Communication has always been a challenge. Dad knew that any discussion regarding values or philosophy begins with the question: "What brings happiness?" One of his primary themes was that the joy of living is in doing: happiness is in accepting, meeting, and conquering life's challenges, and wherever possible doing so for others, not for yourself. Carmack believes that Dad was either influenced by Aristotle's *Nicomachean Ethics*, classifying happiness as an activity, or if not, that his drawing on his own the same conclusions as the great fourth-century B.C. philosopher was even more remarkable.

My father's words strengthened my resolve to accept life and participate actively. Life at times is tough, but happiness is realized by responding to challenges and, if possible, taking care of others in the process, keeping the focus on others rather than on oneself.

⟨⟩⟩⟩

Take It All the Way

Sunday, April 11, 1965

Dear Jay,

It is your birthday—and I haven't forwarded a gift—for which I'm sorry. But I didn't want the day to pass without writing.

I tried to call this morning, but missed you. I'll try again tonight if it's not too late when I get to San Francisco. I'm on my way there to speak to the California Association of Health, Physical Education, and Recreation.

This should be a worthwhile appearance. There will be about 1600 in the meeting. If I can sell them on our Lifetime Sports Program they will be able to move it for us in California—our nation's largest state.

On Tuesday, I'm to speak to the California legislature. "Big Daddy" Unruh will introduce me. I'll actually be giving Casey Conrad an award. However, I'm trying to think of an appropriate political comment or two!

I'll fly home at night on Tuesday to be in the office on Wednesday. Then I'm going on to New York on Thursday to meet with NBC. I've signed my contract for the pre-game show—some "color telecasting"—and some additional appearances. It will be fun and I'm going to try to have you with me on a show or two. If you have any sound, spectacular, interesting ideas as to what you might do, please let me know. I am serious about this.

I cannot let your birthday pass, Jay, without telling you what a great joy you have been for your Dad and Mother. No one could dream of sons like you and Pat—much less actually have them. I regret that we have not been together more—but have a firm premonition that we soon will be. Believe me, you can "take it all the way" in whatever you decide to do—the church, politics, or teaching. And I don't mean this in the worldly sense of popularity and acclaim. Rather, in your own growth, development and what your life will mean to all with whom you come in contact. You have great gifts of spirit, talent, heart and soul. Use them, my son, to their fullest degree!

May this day bring Betty and yourself great happiness. Give lovely Betty my love. We hope to and will see you soon.

> Love always,
> Dad

The Selma to Montgomery civil rights march had just taken place in March 1965. I talked to Mom and Dad on the telephone about the historical significance of the event. We all knew the importance of the cause.

One of my seminarian classmates, Jonathan Daniels, a year ahead of me at ETS, followed Martin Luther King's admonition for clergy and seminarians to participate in the march. Jonathan was there in early March with a small group of other ETS seminarians, when more than five hundred marchers were beaten back with police clubs. Within two weeks the number of demonstrators joining the march had increased fiftyfold to over twenty-five thousand.

There was pressure at ETS within the study body to join the cause. I was motivated to do so. Dr. Joseph Fletcher, the renowned ETS professor of Christian ethics, who himself had been beaten unconscious protesting on behalf of union workers in Cincinnati many years earlier, was very sympathetic to the Selma cause. Yet during a lecture one day he surprised me with his advice when he said, "You people will have many more opportunities—more than you can imagine—to learn to mobilize and to organize for social justice. Your first priority now is to learn the moral imperatives and reasons why you should demonstrate on behalf of justice."

He went on to add, "Following graduation, if you are asked to leave a church during your first two years as a priest, you are not doing your job. You will not have taken time to earn the trust and confidence of your congregation. If you are not asked to leave the same church, after you have been there seven years, you are not doing your job in preaching the gospel!"

Tragically, Daniels was killed in Alabama in August 1965, for his support of the civil rights movement. He had been given permission by the faculty to return after his completion of final exams. Before his death he was active in tutoring children, picketing segregated stores, and integrating the local Episcopal church.

We grieved over Daniels's death. Dad's thoughtful comment on my birthday to "take it all the way," whether in the church or politics or teaching, was a common football metaphor. The phrase has since evolved to "take it to the house," meaning to score a touchdown. He helped me understand that personal success and satisfaction are not defined by one's popularity and acclaim but rather by one's own growth and development and what one gives back to others, supporting them through spirit, talent, heart, and soul.

⊰⊱

On Preparation

1965—Sunday

Dear Jay,

It was good to be with you this past weekend. As always, this time was much too short. We did have a chance to talk a little—but not in nearly enough depth. The shortness of time and interruptions of social duties held us from solidly coming to grips with the realities of life—as best we know them.

Your concern about me and my political future is a bright and wonderful thing to me. It warms my heart, but you must realize that your future is far more important.

Certainly, I wish I had won the election—but I did not. And while many circumstances affected the outcome, the result, and its portent for the future, cannot be altered. I'm a person—who as a candidate— is committed to running as a Republican in a Democratic state. The odds are strongly against me. Perhaps the future will alter the situation—but as of now—one cannot escape the conclusion that I ran at the wrong time on the wrong ticket. My hopes were not fulfilled— but this does not mean I should be depressed—or run again—without an even chance of winning. In all candid honesty, the future is yours—not mine—and I can best serve by helping you.

So at the risk of sounding like a Father again, let me give you my appraisal of the situation. First, I feel you are too concerned about the future—in many respects—and not enough concerned in others. Obviously, this is a paradox. Let me try to explain. You have a sense of duty to the future—but you're not sure what the future will be. You enjoy what you're now doing, but you are not positive it will prove to be pragmatically useful in the future. None of these things should worry you.

European nations admire much about America but they say we lack an understanding in foreign policy. They say we feel we can do whatever the occasion demands—they then explain that foreign relations are like a garden—they take time to grow.

You have total talent. You can do whatever you decide—and there should be no hurry in reaching a decision. Your own wisdom, judgment, and understanding grow each day. Do not be impatient. Your tide will rise and run strongly for you.

I do have a few worries. First, your health. A person is never more effective than his stamina and physical well-being period. Youth can, through its own effervescence, enable you to get along—but over a life-time sound health habits must become a part of your being if you are to develop and use your true potential. Good health is supported by a tri-pod. The three legs are rest, diet, and exercise. Everyone needs 8 hours of sleep each night—a truly balanced diet—with plenty of protein, fresh fruits and vegetables—and each of us needs to exercise each day. In a sense exercise is the key. It makes you rest well, and enhances your appetite.

Please promise yourself—and me that you'll make these basics a habit of your life—each day—from now on.

Your appearance is a factor which is an outgrowth of health habits. Good grooming can be a false front—but as Polonius said, "Apparel oft proclaims the man." Shined shoes—clean shirts—and freshly pressed clothes are not ostentatious. On the contrary, they clearly indicate an individual of fresh outlook—one who is aware, alert and at his best at all times.

My greatest worry, Jay, is about your financial and material outlook. I know the problem is compounded by your studies and your constant awareness of the Christian ethic. The money we spent for dinner today would feed hungry people in many parts of the world for a week! Yet, I feel you should accept certain facts of human existence in this regard.

For a man to function at his best, he needs to be well-rounded—a worker, a student—but in addition he must know joy through recreation in a literal sense. With few exceptions leaders in all walks of life excluding political and religious leaders have lived well in this sense. By so doing they were not being selfish. Rather they were recognizing their humanness—and were re-charging, re-vitalizing their own personal attributes to better contribute to the world during their working hours.

Money and its use remain—and always will remain—one of mankind's great ethical problems. Your desire to be self-sufficient, to not be dependent on me or any one—is a noble, sound attitude. Yet while receiving your education—you should never let such concerns begin to enter your mind. It is a parent's joy—as well as duty—to provide such necessities. If possible, to eliminate monetary worry for their families so they can truly function with the concentration of their total resources on whatever work they undertake.

How far would the Kennedys have come if Old Joe had not made a fortune? Consider the many, many similar examples in our contemporary life.

Living as an athlete has virtue, I am sure, but at your age and development I do not believe it is a practice worthwhile for you.

A proper balance of materialism and intellectual and spiritual growth and development is one of life's most difficult adjustments. My advice, for what it's worth, is to live fully and well—as you emotionally and physically feel you should—without worry, concern or guilt feelings of any kind about what you do—and whether or not your associates can or cannot do more or less than you do.

I did not take the Foundation job only because of money—which would be helpful to us all. In view of all the circumstances we discussed, it was the wisest decision. I had no opportunities in Oklahoma which would help me live politically and the jobs offered did not contain much public service or personal challenge. In my present work, I have freedom to set my own course—make my own decisions in a job which has great over tones of National need. In addition, my football TV will keep me deeply involved with the game I know and love. If and when the political scene changes I can run again.

But, let me repeat, you and your future are the keys to tomorrow. Prepare yourself carefully and well. Don't force the situation. Let the warm sense of learning and experience ripen and sharpen your intellect and attitudes. And so your mind may function at its best, eat well, exercise and rest soundly each night.

Have balance in your life of study, expression, prayer, service, fun, recreation, and frivolity. Look sharp and feel sharp—the future belongs to you. It will be brighter than the stars.

All my love,
Dad

Dad had agreed to head up and be spokesperson for the Lifetime Sports Foundation sponsored by AMF and Brunswick. He was interested in creating more opportunities for people to develop competence in a sport they could enjoy forever. Initially, Brunswick and AMF were focused exclusively on the promotion of bowling as a lifetime activity, but Dad wanted to expand the program to include golf, tennis, and other lifetime sports.

We had dined the previous week at an expensive restaurant in Boston, enjoying a four-course gourmet meal. I felt guilty about Dad's spending money at a lavish restaurant on ourselves instead of using it for a more practical purpose, such as giving it to the indigent. He acknowledged that a proper balance of spiritual growth and materialism was a "difficult adjustment." On the one hand, giving to those less fortunate was a duty and responsibility. On the other hand, he justified joy through recreation as a means of recharging my batteries in order to contribute better to the world. He did not believe I should feel guilty or that our behavior was selfish; on the contrary, he thought almost all leaders in all professions—including religious leaders—had lived well in that sense throughout history. He helped me understand that leaders can be more effective in serving others by taking time to refocus in a relaxed atmosphere than by never taking time to enjoy themselves.

At ETS, as in most academic environments, it was customary and acceptable to wear informal baggy clothes without shined shoes. Dad quoted Shakespeare's Polonius to make his point about this. The qualities of neatness, order, and self-discipline learned from his father C.P., during his years at Shattuck Military Academy, and in the U.S. Navy were ingrained in his mind. It was clear to me that he did not like my dress code. OU football players were expected to dress well on and off the field, and Dad saw a positive correlation between one's dress appearance and overall performance. While sympathetic to his standards, I continued to conform to the more relaxed dress code during my three years in graduate school.

He encouraged me to be patient in making a final determination about my vocation and suggested I was too concerned about the future and not enough about others. He affirmed my enjoyment of studies as part of the preparation process to provide a moral and intellectual foundation on which to build, regardless of vocation. His advice had a calming effect that gave me confidence about the validity of my studies.

Father's Footsteps

8/11/1965—Monday

Dear Jay and Betty,

Thank you so much for the book. Believe me, I need it! It is the type of reference work which I will keep in my office and refer to at frequent intervals.

I hope your week and holiday was fun. I'm delighted you are finally getting a chance to see more of beautiful New England.

When you have a moment, Jay, call John Yovicsin of Harvard. I have written him about your interest in coaching and he will be expecting your call. We will talk to you on the phone over the week-end to make arrangements about the car.

Love always,
Dad

During my second semester in graduate school I decided to become a graduate assistant football coach. Dad had assisted in contacting the Harvard head football coach, John Yovicsin, but I ended up coaching for two years at Boston University (BU) for Head Coach Warren Schmakel.

It was a rewarding and meaningful experience to assist the BU freshman football team in a game I understood so well. I enjoyed the return to the sounds of colliding football pads, the smell of grass and locker rooms, repetition of drills, and plain execution on the field. Football coaching would have been a profession I would have enjoyed, having learned it easily from my father and

Duke coach Bill Murray. Since for many years I had lived a coach's life vicariously, I was motivated to consider a different profession, from which I hoped I could provide service to others and find satisfaction in the process.

I spent the summer working in a geriatrics ward at Boston State Mental Hospital as a seminarian assistant, with other classmates at ETS who worked in other departments at the hospital. This education was part of ETS's direction, throwing seminarians into the reality of life and death and situations probably not experienced before but that would later become routine responsibilities for priests or laymen of the church.

The experience forced me to comprehend the sadness and void that so many feel at final stages of life, especially with the loss of mental faculties. The obvious question of how a loving God could allow such an unsettling end to human life became a daily recurrence for me. It was the same question Dad had asked when sailors on the *Enterprise* were killed during World War II. It was the same question he asked about why some paratroopers were saved in Europe during the war while others were killed; a question for the centuries. We were willing to take the leap of faith that God, a living, loving spirit and the force behind the creation of the universe, permitted both good and evil. But it is a leap of faith.

Beyond learning how to care for older patients with or without mental issues, the key takeaway for me was learning the importance of listening. We were taught that much psychological healing was simply being with people—not talking to them—but being with them in their own feelings—sorrow, pain, suffering, or just getting along. The natural tendency for humans was to talk in those situations; I came to understand the importance of silence when building trust between people.

A Perspective on Loss

11-2-1965—Tuesday

Dear Jay and Betty,

It has been a long time since I've written—and again I apologize. Today, I dictated a short letter which Kathy probably didn't get out as yet. In it I'll enclose your medical history letter from Mayo's for the draft board—and a bill which I hope you've paid.

Yesterday Boston Smith called to tell Mother that Harrison had died. I was in New York and couldn't get the message until last night. The funeral was today at 4 P.M. There simply was no way I could get there—but I was sad and disappointed. He was a true friend to me in every way. If you have a moment I think it would be good to write his son, Boston. The address is 1524 Camden Way, Oklahoma City.

The pre-game show on Regional networks is much more time-consuming. I'll do one show from the top—and then three more openings—3rd segment—and summary. The producer and the crew are getting in the groove though and everything moves much more smoothly. I haven't forgotten about your talent fee, Jay—and will forward it shortly.

It's sad to talk to the losing coaches each week. Darrell Royal is still battling hard—but shocked to say the least. They've had so many injuries they haven't had their offensive unit together in practice. In the last three games they've lost the ball 14 times on fumbles and interceptions. It's obvious this is why they've lost.

We have Alabama and LSU this week which should be great. I'm looking forward to seeing Bear and plan to have dinner with him on Friday.

We're looking forward to the Army Navy weekend!!

> Always my love, always
> Dad

The Vietnam War intensified during the mid-1960s and impacted all male youth in their twenties. After suffering bleeding ulcers in college and being hospitalized twice, I was declared 1-Y (a deferment) by the draft board. Dad helped provide my medical history and made sure that all medical bills were paid.

Boston Smith, a federal judge in Oklahoma City, was the son of Dad's close friend Harrison Smith, a character whose valet always teed up his golf ball and picked up his ball from the cup after he holed out a putt! Harrison was one of the biggest supporters of the Touchdown Club, a group of wealthy boosters who raised money to support the OU athletic program. Oklahoma was placed on probation for two years between 1954 and 1956 when an NCAA Infractions Committee found the club guilty of buying clothes and paying medical expenses for wives and children of student-athletes. In *Presidents Can't Punt* George Cross stated that no serious charges against the university had been sustained, and OU was not precluded from bowl competition. Dad was angry and thought the university had upheld all conference policies, but he said nothing publicly.

One evening in 1959 Pat and I joined Dad for dinner at Harrison's home, after which we went to watch the heavyweight championship boxing match between Ingemar Johansson and Floyd Patterson televised live at the Civic Center auditorium in downtown Oklahoma City. Johansson was victorious with a surprise first-round knockout.

On the drive home Harrison told a story about another first-round knockout. He traveled to Europe in the 1930s, long before the age of jet aircraft travel, to observe a championship fight. It was an exhausting trip, and as he settled into his front-row seat at ringside and lowered his head to light a cigar, the bell rang to begin the first round. Within an instant his companion hollered, "He's down; he's down!" One of the boxers had been knocked out. Harrison had traveled all the way to Europe and had not seen one blow!

⋘⋙

A Life Spent in Service

11-16-1965—Monday Night

Dear Jay,

It was good to talk with you last night. I wish you could have been with us—but it is comforting to know we will be together soon.

Believe me, I can fully understand your concern about the future. Here I am almost 50 years old and still much in doubt myself as to what I should do. I have always envied and admired people like John Kirklin and Bill Sauer—and Pat, who at an early age were sure what they wanted to do. Once this decision is reached—everything, if you have reasonable talent—and are willing to work hard—should be down hill.

In your case, I don't think you should try to force anything. God, in his good time, will assist you in making decisions—when they need to be made.

If you feel you are learning now—that you're becoming a more mature person with an ever deepening understanding of life and its complexities—I don't believe you should be concerned about anything else. On the other hand—if you're not happy in school—and don't feel the time spent is worthwhile—you should plan to do something else next semester. The decision should be made in June—and if you're back to school in the fall—again in January next year.

Above all don't feel any compulsion or pressure to stay in school if you aren't satisfied.

So far as playing football is concerned, my feelings are unchanged. If the challenge is there—if you aren't going to be happy—or to feel a sense of complete fulfillment unless you give it a try—then by all means you should. However—unless this is a sincere personal challenge—a testing of yourself—I think you would be foolish to play.

If you don't want to go to school—you could coach—work at a job—maybe take a trip abroad—while reading and studying on your own. What I'm really saying is that no one but yourself can make the decision as to what course of life will give you a sense of being needed—of accomplishment—and satisfaction.

If you decide you want to try Pro ball—there will be no need to worry about when you tell Kansas City and the Bears. When the decision is made, simply call them and tell them. Your decision one way or the other won't change their draft selections this year. I don't believe you should raise their hopes that you might play—until you are sure you will.

Just one other thing, don't let money alter your decision in any way. I'm making more money than I ever dreamed I would—and I've also saved quite a bit. You have no economic pressures. To even the cost of your education with Pat's would necessitate your spending about $3,200 a year for about six years. I don't believe in handling money exactly in this fashion—but mention it only to point out that you should—sincerely feel free from the necessity of doing anything simply for the money involved. Money is only good to spend—and you have all you need for now at least.

Life should, I believe, be spent in service in some worthwhile cause or endeavor which brings you satisfaction and joy in the process of accomplishment. Many, many professions and jobs fill this definition.

The important thing is to do—to the best of your ability—whatever you do. Comedians have their important role to play. Laughter is needed in life. Who is to say they do not contribute as much as a scholastic or scholar?

Life is ever changing and it always will continue to. The great truths remain—but social conditions and man's scientific progress will continue to alter our way of life. One adage which is on point—"the only time you must not fail—is the last time you try" can be applied to all who in questioning their course of action—try several different professions—or many different solutions to the same problem.

I've rambled on at length, but I sense a concern in your mind that you should not feel. Take things as they come—in stride—make what seems to be the sensible wise decision *when the time for decision is at hand.* This is all anyone can actually do. To fret and fuss over what decision you might make before you actually are in position to make a choice is truly a foolish waste of time.

We can talk at length, I hope, at the Army-Navy game. It will be so good to see you. Give Betty our love. We're truly proud of you both.

All my love, always,
Dad

P.S. If the writing is shaky at times it's because I'm flying from New York to Washington and the plane has had a few bumps.

Am enclosing your check for the pre-game show. You can forward it for deposit—or just cash it—Hope we can do more trips like this together in the future.

Dad continued to provide thoughtful advice to help me understand the best way to decide my future. My primary interest remained in Christian social ethics, but the pursuit of a career as a priest in the Episcopal Church still was not clear to me.

Dr. John Kirklin and Dr. Bill Sauer were Dad's good friends for many years. Sauer was a leading medical internist at the Mayo Clinic, and Kirklin, Dad's fraternity brother at the University of Minnesota, became a renowned cardiac surgeon at the Mayo Clinic and later headed that department at the University of Alabama at Birmingham Medical Center. Dad's envy of people like them and my brother Pat, who at early ages were sure what they wanted to do, made me chuckle because Dad also knew at an early age what he wanted to do. He wanted to coach. The difference was that he had left the coaching profession after a distinguished seventeen-year career as OU head coach to enter politics. After his loss in the U.S. Senate race at the age of forty-eight, he was in a predicament similar to mine, except that he was nearing fifty, not in his early twenties.

Reflecting on his advice made it clearer to me that it did little good to agonize over decisions before they actually had to be made. I believed in the spiritual power of prayer and its impact in the decision-making process. We agreed that I should do my best to trust God and his spirit without trying to control the spirit. Dad stressed that simplicity and tolerance were important—as was being practical.

Nagging second thoughts about my turning down a professional football career surfaced from time to time. Dad once again advised me that the only reason to play was if there was a sincere personal challenge to test myself—which there was not. He stressed the need to make a decision that gave a sense of satisfaction for life lived in a worthwhile manner and bringing joy and accomplishment. His continual emphasis on the importance of service to others and doing my best regardless of the profession was affirming. Accomplishments are fulfilled in many different ways. As alternatives were available, I agreed that the only time I must not fail was that last time I tried.

Duffy Daugherty

Spring 1966

Dear Jay and Betty,

My birthday present was wonderful!! Thank you so much for your thoughtfulness. I haven't been in circumstances where I could try for ½ a yard—but hope I will soon.

Did you read the historical note on the glass? I was interested to learn that the glasses were designed during Elizabethan days to hand up to the man driving the coach without spilling any of the beer. He was so high they needed the tall glass so he could reach down for it while still holding the reins for the horses.

Spent Monday and Tuesday at East Lansing filming Michigan State for next fall's TV show. They have some super athletes—but they don't appear to have the best organized practice I've ever seen. Duffy is such a fine, funny, warm man. It's a joy to be around him.

For example, he had Andy Kerr who's now 87, out for this week as his guest to watch practice—and talk football.

Am planning to be in Baltimore Saturday night for the Pithotomy Club Show. I hope your brother doesn't embarrass me with his ribald songs. Dave and Happy are driving over with me.

You're in my thoughts always—it will be wonderful to see you again in a few weeks.

> All my love,
> Dad

PS: Could you forward another copy of *Situation Ethics* so I could send it to Francie Daugherty. We had a most interesting discussion of it. She's a formal, devout Catholic. Nuff said?

We celebrated Dad's birthday at the Yard of Ale restaurant in Harvard Square, where beer and ale were consumed in extra-tall glasses. He was fascinated by the inscription and pondered its historical significance.

He displayed an element of humor by commenting on some social time with Pat, who was still a medical student at Johns Hopkins. The Pithotomy Club was a medical fraternity created for members of the Johns Hopkins medical community to enjoy meals and parties and generate camaraderie. One of its most eagerly anticipated events, frequented by prestigious Hopkins doctors, was its annual show of hilariously vulgar, crude, and irreverent skits performed by medical students. Dad was kidding about possible embarrassment; he knew such events fostered close-knit relationships.

His request for Joseph Fletcher's book *Situation Ethics* for Duffy Daugherty's wife Francie was due to our ongoing conversations. Fletcher was a distinguished and much-published ethicist who later became Virginia Medical School's first professor of bioethics. Fletcher believed complex moral questions cannot be answered with oversimplifications or micro-ethics. Moral decision making requires broad fact finding on many subjects. His writings suggest that when a Christian becomes involved in a social problem, basic questions must be addressed regarding theological issues at stake and Christian imperatives relevant to the issue.

The Harvard Business School is well known for using the Socratic method of teaching through questions, and Fletcher enjoyed teaching at HBS on the process and strategy of reaching just and ethical solutions to business, economic, and health care issues. Dad never tired of debates on case studies providing better understanding of ethical conclusions to complex situations.

⋘⋙

On Financial Planning

April 25, 1966

Dear Jay and Betty,

It was good to talk with you last night. You both sounded well and happy. I'm pleased, Betty, that you are planning to fly home. You definitely should. I know how much your folks want to see you.

The coming week will be routine travel for me. I don't know how I get so involved—but guess it is the problem of being booked for occasional dates far in advance. Then when I fill in the gaps—I find myself like this week—going to Buch Hill Falls, Pennsylvania, Garden City, Kansas, and West Palm Beach, Florida.

I think we told you about Mom's investment course. She went to class and I read the books. Anyway, I've known for a long time I should take a more active interest in our investments. Mom's teacher is also a broker. We had her check our accounts and make recommendations. Am enclosing a card which lists yours as they now are. I believe it would be a good thing if you followed them once a week or so. Potter & Statham Investments is on the American Exchange, Trans-International Airlines is over the counter, the others are on the New York Stock Exchange.

We are looking forward to the end of May when we'll be with you again.

Always my love,
Dad

Dad learned about money from his father, who was the head of the Wilkinson Finance Company. Later as OU director of athletics Dad was responsible for the entire OU sports program and all financial reports within the department. While he never relished a position as chief financial officer, he understood the basics required to administer any business venture or program.

For his personal investments his approach was conservative and relied heavily on bank investment professionals. The explosion of mutual fund growth was in its infancy, and he preferred to select diversified individual stocks rather than purchasing shares in mutual funds. He maintained an active interest in oil and gas ventures and worked closely with Norman geologist Gene Culp to take small positions in oil and gas investments throughout the state. Because Dad's name was so well known, speculators hounded him to lend his name to drilling ventures. He never felt comfortable with an oil or gas investment unless the lead promoter had himself taken a substantial financial position in the venture.

Dad and Duffy Daugherty's Coach-of-the-Year clinics were organized to provide meaningful information to as many high school coaches as possible. They later became profitable ventures based on a formula of splitting the revenue with the twelve clinic managers.

⋐⋑⋐⋑

Predicting the Decline

Spring 1966—Wednesday

Dear Jay,

It was good to get your thoughtful, perceptive letter. The breadth of your educational and personal experience is the best possible preparation you can have for whatever future you decide to make.

The courses you are having in Public Administration should be studied in a simplified form by all citizens. Had I possessed a better understanding, and had I been actively engaged sooner, perhaps I could have been a more effective citizen.

I am constantly amazed and dismayed by the success of the political appeal to selfishness. Politicians do not create wealth. Yet their success seems measured by what they "do or give" to their constituents. If the most successful politician (office holder) is the one who gets, for his district, the biggest cut of the pie—you have created, as we have, a situation where the recipients are profiting at the expense of others.

Citizens should know that they are part of a whole. To demand more than a fair share—and elect men who presumably can achieve this false goal—will ultimately destroy our initiative and self-reliance as a nation.

Socialism in theory is sound. In practice it has a stifling effect. In our era of geological time and state of evolution, too many people will take the easy way if the opportunity is granted.

I have thought a bit about your term paper topic. If you did want to write on a contemporary subject, you might consider the Kerr vs. Roy Turner Sensational Democratic Primary.

My memory is somewhat sketchy but, generally speaking, the situation developed as follows: Kerr was Governor during the early war years. I believe Turner succeeded him as Governor, Turner was much more popular than Kerr—and probably was a better Governor. He ran against Kerr for the Senate after Kerr's first term. There were three primary candidates. Neither man gained a majority which necessitated a run-off. Both were wealthy men. Mid-way in the primary campaign Turner withdrew because he couldn't "afford" to continue the race. The hidden factors are obvious—and would be interesting.

Coincidentally, while I'm no expert in political theory or practice—I know a considerable amount about conducting a campaign—in a practical sense.

Your summer plans sound excellent. I have a limited understanding of slums and poverty—because as a coach—you don't experience it in depth. An analysis of the "why" is vital here—and probably grossly misunderstood. Is it lack of fortune and talent or unfortunate circumstances? For the second and third generation, I'd go for the circumstance factor—but not in the first generation. What do you think? The importance of early childhood training is probably the key to not losing more people—but how do we do it?

One other comment in your letter was of great interest—"3rd and 4th generation [century] phraseology used to articulate the faith keeping people from the church." This is actually becoming a distressingly real factor to me. I want to go to church—but so much of it is so unrealistic and formalized that I become frustrated. What can be done here to improve the situation?

It has been said often—but it remains true—that religion should be lived constantly—in our waking hours seven days a week. We should not pay observance as an insurance policy for slightly more than one hour per week and feel we are living the faith.

There is so much we need to discuss—I need to learn from you—and hopefully my experience can be of help to you

Jack told us Betty was reading many more books about care—feeding prenatal considerations for the mother, etc. You and Betty will be the finest of parents. Teasingly, but seriously, the baby will develop eating habits based on parental conduct. That's why I'm glad, Betty dear—that you're on the vegetable, fruit, and protein plan—instead of sweets!!

Mom joins in sending our love. We're looking forward to Easter and to talking to you soon.

Love always,

Dad

Betty was within one month of delivering our daughter Kirsten on October 2, 1966. My cousin Jack Ransom, a Georgetown law student, briefed Mom and Dad on Betty's dietary plans, and Dad could not pass up that opportunity to put in a good word for properly balanced diets.

One major reason his OU football teams achieved such remarkable success was that players learned to subordinate individual goals for the good of the team. When a cause transcended individual recognition, he taught, a team had an excellent chance for success. He saw United States citizens too as part of a whole, part of a country, and therefore part of a team. As a coach he knew that some players would choose the easy way out and not pay the price to help a team achieve success. If a political system offered benefits without the requirement of citizens giving something back, he believed many people would react selfishly. If it encouraged politicians to deliver pork barrel projects at the expense of others, inequity was created in the system. The lesson is as real as when he wrote the letter almost fifty years ago.

During my second summer in graduate school I worked as a housing inspector for the City of Boston to assist tenants in the Roxbury, Dorchester, and South End areas. Growing up in Oklahoma I had never encountered poverty and slums, and it was a shock to understand the sharp contrast between the affluent and the poor. My first reaction was that if everyone had an opportunity to experience those deplorable conditions, there would be no argument about these people desperately needing help. Within a day I modified that position, realizing that the worst apartments were often located next to others in excellent condition. The physical condition of the apartment seemed to depend on a tenant's ability to take responsibility for its upkeep.

That summer I learned that the problems were far more complex than I had originally imagined, and solutions were not always tied to money alone, since many people had not been taught appropriate values for keeping property from destruction. I also became more convinced that Christian and other faith-based groups had a clear obligation and moral responsibility to reach out to others in need.

⊰⊱~⊰⊱

On Politics and Professions

6/3/1966—Thursday night

Dear Jay,

As always it was wonderful to be with you. Yet somehow, with other people always around our problem communicating deeply is difficult. I feel we grow in perception, but that it is largely the result of empathy—not a true rational exchange of ideas.

Since leaving last night I've given a great deal of thought to your concern about your running for office—or my running. I don't believe it's exactly either-or, but would like to set forth my ideas so far as both of us are concerned. When I see you next we can discuss the situation carefully and candidly. At the outset let me make it perfectly clear (This is strange stationery for a serious letter!!) that I am not trying to influence you in any way to enter politics as a career. Rather, I would like you to analyze the pros and cons as I see them from my limited experience.

My career as a football coach taught me many things—but most of all to be a practical realist. In this world, I believe this method of evaluation is essential.

Success in politics for any individual requires many attributes. The major ones as I see them are:

1. A well known name.
2. An acceptable, proper image in the minds of the voting public.
3. A personality that identifies favorably with the aspirations of the majority of one's constituents.
4. A "feel" for the projected hopes and political desires of a majority of one's constituents.
5. The ability to do one's homework. To study—reflect—and know in what one believes. From the base can be projected the programs designed to accomplish one's objectives. This requires, obviously, work, study—and then courage in execution.
6. A political base from which to launch one's career. Bob Kennedy is an example of a successful politician who in New York had no normal base—but as a brother of a revered, assassinated President—he had a base almost anywhere that was legal.
7. Adequate financing of two kinds. First, the ability to support one's family properly. Secondly, the resources to conduct a campaign without becoming beholden to anyone because of their financial help.

In relating these items to myself, I am adequate in 1, 2, and 6—deficient in the others.

As a Republican in Oklahoma, I miss on #3 solely on party ground. The same is true of #4.

#5 is perhaps my biggest handicap. I feel my judgment—given the facts—is satisfactory—but during the last campaign I lacked the ability to arrange my study schedule—or to develop a staff to supply me with the facts on which sound decisions could be made.

During the last campaign #7 was no problem—but for me it would have been were I a candidate now in '66.

As I view your situation, you can qualify well under every item I have listed. Item #5 would be the most troublesome. Talk is so easy and cheap. The temptation to talk around a problem—instead of coming to grips with it—basing conclusions on false, antiquated statistics is so simple compared to a totally current analysis—that this mental self-discipline is, I believe, the point of separation between success and failure. You could do this with no trouble—but only if you were willing to "pay the price" in self-discipline.

Frankly, I'm a better coach than player. I say this candidly. It was true in college—and athletically since. For example, I believe my advice made the difference in Jim Hewgley's winning his election. Thus, I'm inclined to treat politics as I have football.

My present work is stimulating and provides an excellent income. To digress for a moment, my main concern over my current activities is the fact that I'm paid so well. I wonder if I'm not "going along" because of the dollars involved. For example, my TV contract will be for about $35,000 which is about $10,000 more than I would make as a College Coach with all of the pressures and uncertainties of the job. I don't feel I'm selling out—but I am concerned about being dollar conscious instead of spending my life purposefully—and meaningfully.

My practical political situation can be concisely analyzed. As a Republican in a traditionally Democratic state I open the game with all the odds against me. Perhaps, I could be elected Governor—but frankly, I lack the knowledge and experience to administer a state—even though I do feel adequate to represent Oklahoma. Also, my age precludes my starting in politics, a basic simple assignment—the years would run out before I hit the big time—which to me means an office in a large enough [state] to give one a true ability to influence the course of major events.

Your situation is dramatically different. You begin with a fine name (which you have made yourself) and you hold the warm reputation which goes with this.

You are young enough to serve the necessary years of apprentice-ship and learning to prepare you for any assignment.

Depending on where you make your political base you can choose your own party. In this instance, I would recommend a careful analysis of the "pendulum factor" in American political history.

One party, or the other, has been in control for a reasonable span of years—but the tide has always changed. Perhaps it will again. This should be a cold, calculated decision since within each party you could find many who hold to your own philosophy.

Financially, if I continue my present activities, you will have no problems. Please don't take this statement in the wrong way. Money is useful only to spend in a worthwhile manner. Making money is a combination of luck, circumstance, and ability. I happen to have stumbled into a good thing. The best use of my good fortune would be to use these funds in a worthy cause.

As you carefully consider your career, I would add that you must recognize the restrictions of living which are imposed on a politician, and you must decide if you are willing to accept these restrictive circumstances.

Your family will literally live in a fish bowl (witness the Johnson sisters). You will be forced to spend many evenings and a reasonable number of daylight hours with people with whom you have no normal bonds except that they are helpful politically. Actually, you may not like them at all.

The judgments of the public will severely limit your social activities. To be honestly on top of your job will require countless hours of open-minded study and analysis of the changing domestic and foreign problems with which our nation is confronted.

There is one other point which should be mentioned. Politically, one's contribution is environmental—not personal. There is little personal, individual contact with people where you realize clearly you have changed this life (as I occasionally did as a coach). Instead, you may change and affect many lives through your activities, but you will not know or personally realize which individuals were touched or benefited in which ways. This impersonal factor is not as satisfying as a direct contact with an individual.

I don't want to end the letter with an attempt to give advice or draw conclusions. Were I to do so, I feel I would be unduly imposing my own ideas—instead of freely allowing you to draw your own conclusions.

Perhaps the best thing would be for you to save this letter—and when I see you at Pat's graduation we can go off alone together and discuss it point by point.

In analyzing any job—let alone the choice of career—these points, I believe, are essential:

1. Are the responsibilities sufficient to test your talents?
2. Do you have an opportunity to fully utilize your own initiative—to make your own unique contribution?
3. Does the activity give you an opportunity to serve others? To turn outward givingly—not inward selfishly?
4. Most important, does the activity bring you personal happiness and satisfaction? One must be happy on a day to day basis to do anything well.

Your potential is unlimited. I truly mean this. Don't set your sights low. Follow your fondest star—but make practical plans as to how you will reach it.

Many people—in fact the majority of people—*react* to events. They never *cause* things to happen. Only by defining your goals—planning how to achieve them—and preparing properly is it possible to *cause* things to happen your way—instead of *reacting* to events stimulated by others. This approach to life is the only one which brings satisfaction over a period of time. It is a matter of riding with the tides and current—as opposed to setting sail and steering your own course.

Give Betty my love. It was wonderful to be with you—and it will be even better to see you both again in a couple of weeks.

All my love,
Dad

This comprehensive, substantive, and realistic assessment of politics as a profession was written on stationery from the Flying Carpet Motor Inn in Des Plaines, Illinois. Former Oklahoma governor and U.S. senator Henry Bellmon later told me he agreed that Dad was a better political adviser than candidate. Bellmon felt Dad did not really enjoy the comfort of the crowds he was required to be with as a candidate.

Living in a fishbowl was not new. As sons of an iconic father, Pat and I were always under scrutiny. Yet it is true that demands and sacrifices are heavy for people in public life and that it takes commitment to stay abreast of critical domestic and international issues. The similarity and parallels between politics and football were obvious—one had to have the will to win and be willing to "pay the price in self-discipline" to be successful—a belief that was a cornerstone of Dad's philosophy. His themes of preparation and goal setting also modeled his principles for success in athletics and once again affirmed my confidence in what I had learned on the playing field.

Upon graduation from ETS, I was ordained as a deacon in the Episcopal Church in 1967 and worked part-time at St. John's in Norman. My full-time job was executive assistant to Oklahoma governor Dewey Bartlett, representing him on boards and commissions and accompanying him in travel throughout the state. Within a year I joined Nixon's presidential campaign and, after his election, worked on the White House staff for one year as a staff assistant to the president, reporting to H. R. Haldeman, White House chief of staff.

Later I decided to return to Oklahoma to run for the 4th Congressional District, with 90 percent registered Democrats and 10 percent registered Republicans, against a twenty-four-year incumbent. We knew it would not be easy, and any mistake could be fatal to election results. I hired a Chicago advertising agency run by Jim Brady, who was later White House press secretary to President Ronald Reagan and seriously injured in John Hinckley Jr.'s assassination attempt on the president in 1981.

One of our thirty-second advertisements showed me walking through a cow pasture looking up to the sky, with quiet music overtones interacting with a peaceful visual of cattle in the background. An announcer's voice softly said, "Jay Wilkinson gives all he's got and more!" That was it. My opponent Tom Steed poked fun at me, saying, "I may not be as smart as that young whippersnapper Wilkinson, but I have enough common sense to know when walking through a cow pasture, I better look down to see that I don't step in anything instead of looking up in the sky!" Steed's comment resonated with voters and my ad proved a costly mistake. It was later featured in Jack Anderson's nationally syndicated column "Washington Merry-Go-Round." My sad lesson: we had not properly vetted the advertisement. It was a lack of preparation.

I ran a solid campaign for the U.S. Congress but lost. The Wilkinsons were 0–2 in races for elected national office. I pondered whether it had been wise to leave a profession I knew and understood so well—football.

Selflessness

6/26/1966

Dear Jay and Betty,

I'm on my way from St. Louis to San Diego—the names recognize our Nation's Christian heritage—and I am lonely and wondering, as I constantly do of my purpose—my possible contribution to society. As yet I have no solid answer or conviction.

It is a beautiful flight. We left at 6:30—it is now 8:30—but we've been traveling with "sunset on the clouds" all the way.

The American desert is vast. On the surface of the ground, I'm sure it's not beautiful. Rather, it is hot, dusty, forbidding land where only serpents, insects, and lizards eke out a precarious existence. The courage of the pioneers in crossing the country was remarkable. Probably it was made possible by the "richness of the goal"—which in this case was the gold of California.

Regardless of why they started, their achievements have built a great country. Essentially, the fuel for such performance must come from the heart. As the challenge to go West has been recognized by Historians—"The Cowards never started, and the weak died on the way"—is simply further recognition of the demand for excellence in a world of evolution. The status quo is an admission of defeat. We must find better solutions to all our problems. With research, honesty and high hope—I believe we can.

Our unique experiment in Government has made the nation the finest (not the strongest, most arrogant or most domineering) the world has yet known. We have freely given more of our substance to help others achieve not only economic prosperity—but also military parity.

Why? Because of our faith in God. We "are"—perhaps "were" would be a better term—a Nation that based our actions on an honest conviction in the reality of God and his judgment. It was the faith that triggered our experiment in pure democracy.

As the philosopher Hocking pointed out, "Democracy is the most difficult and perilous form of government because it calls for unselfishness on the part of officers and voters alike. To sustain this high morality against the tide requires religion—because it is only religion that makes morality a command from the cosmos."

This, Jay, perhaps is your task.

In a limited way I was able to achieve through my coaching a momentary selflessness on the part of our team. When we played well, it was because the cause transcended individual recognition or honor.

You possess the quality to teach this to the nation—and to the world.

I don't say this lightly—I mean it—and my opinion is based on practical experience in the world of leadership.

We must get away for a few days where quietly and without interruption, we can talk, think, perfect, reflect, and formulate the best use of our allotted years.

While Pat's graduation was fun and worthy of a celebration, I know we both need less artificial stimulation of glamorous restaurants, entertainment, and wine. Instead we should seek quiet to chart our course.

I love you both and am looking forward to spending next Tuesday with you.

Always,
Dad

From this letter alone, one sees Dad's interests ranging from geology to evolution; from American history to philosophy; from political science to religion to football. His active mind was focused on diverse subjects yet always reflected his special qualities: he was a man of service; he believed that as individuals and as a nation, Americans were constantly being challenged and evolving in our pursuit of excellence; and our faith in God was an important factor in our individual lives and our country's history.

Throughout his life he demonstrated a commitment to being of service to others. Yet in this letter he wrote about being lonely and wondering what his future contribution to society might be. The statement shows genuine humility and exemplifies his great desire to serve. Two years after losing his Senate race he was still restive.

Dad watched as our nation moved in a secular direction but always maintained that faith in God was an important ingredient in its growth and development. His own religious beliefs were rather simple. He believed that we were created by a loving God and, as Ralph Waldo Emerson expressed it, that our purpose was to leave the world a little better than we found it. He considered himself a follower of Jesus and his commandments to love God with all your heart, mind, and soul, and love your neighbor as yourself. And he always felt a closeness between the world of nature and human nature, and that God was revealed in each day's sunrise and sunset and in all of nature, just as in the Old and New Testaments.

He believed that football and all sports help participants to understand life in general with all of its ups and downs—to understand the important values of life that are inherent in sports, such as selflessness, self-discipline, preparation, sacrifice, commitment, courage, overcoming adversity, and giving back to others for a cause larger than any one person. It was easy to see why he had been so committed to his earlier profession as a coach.

❧❧

Perfect Answers

9/1966—Monday Night

Dear Jay and Betty,

It was good to be with you on Thursday. As always, I regret that we seem so caught up in the world and with people that we didn't have the opportunity to leisurely talk about important ideas. We must soon. I can learn much from you—and hopefully, pass on to you the knowledge of my experience.

You were excellent on the TV program!! The people at NBC were most pleased. Everyone I talked with thought the show was good—but Mom thought they photographed you from the wrong side!

This week I have Texas vs. Arkansas which should be a great game. Mom and I were going home over the weekend, but Oklahoma is playing so poorly, I'm embarrassed to. Grandmother hasn't been feeling too well, so Mother is flying to Grinnell Thursday to spend a week with her. She'll meet me at South Bend for the Notre Dame–USC game the next Friday. I'll spend Saturday night with Jim Hewgley.

I'm so disappointed OU isn't playing better—but actually I'm not surprised. With their backs like Hart and Brown they ought to score—and should make some yardage. Against Texas they didn't make a single first down in the first half and had only 27 yards gained. I'm afraid it will be a bitter experience for Gomer.

Duke played well against Pitt. Everyone wanted to be remembered to you. Glacken is a fine player. If they can be tough enough on defense, they could go all the way. Calabrese has amazing speed. I have the perfect 1-on-1 defense for the swing end, but will keep the secret to myself until the season ends!!

Your courses sound excellent and I'm sure you'll gain much insight, understanding, and wisdom this year. You should face the fundamental questions openly and unafraid. There are few inclusive perfect answers, but if anyone can develop them—I'm sure it will be you.

In my view, the acceptance of—and successful meeting of—the "challenge" is a basic quality of human existence and progress. Here in America we have almost reached the saturation point in meeting the material challenge of living. The majority of the world, however, remains poor and hungry.

I'm not sure of the cause or meaning of "challenge" but can explain its mystery and pertinence to mankind. To overcome space and the ocean depths is a current challenge. To defeat other men athletically or in the classroom is another example of the same idea—as is the challenge of nations against nations.

Most important of all is the personal challenge of how we live our lives. What can we do to make the world better? What is significant action personally? Can we be true to the best that is within us? Or will we succumb to selfishness?

These are things I need to talk over with you—and of course there are many more.

Mother and I are so proud of you both—Betty keep eating well. Promise? We'll talk to you soon.

Love always,
Dad

PS: Was pleased B.U. won Saturday. Your presence is really helping.

Dad always took a particular interest in my theological studies. In discussions we agreed that there was no difference between what a Christian person and any other person of the twentieth century did. Both participated in the issues and events of the day and both might have arrived at the same conclusions. The difference was an inner one—a faith-based concern. He believed personal moral and ethical challenges—the elevation of our obligation to be unselfish—were the most important of all.

I was thrilled to hear about my former teammates in his telecast of the Duke-Pittsburgh game. He shared remembrances and joked about keeping to himself the secret of the perfect defense for the Duke swing end. Duke was committed to its offensive philosophy that when our wide receiver (swing end) was not covered by two defensive players, the Duke quarterback would call for a specific pass play thrown to the swing end. It worked very well for several years. Our debates were enjoyable and humorous, evoking Dad's remark in his first letter when I was a freshman at Duke that sometimes the approach of other teams could "get the job done more effectively—maybe more easily than we can."

Dad was quite comfortable on television. During the football season his live Sunday afternoon coach's shows were watched by Sooner fans throughout the state, as he used his small magnetic "little men" to illustrate specific plays and features of the games. He also hosted the first syndicated sports program, *Sports for the Family*. Dad had an uncanny sense of timing and felt at ease looking into the camera, describing the process to me as "thinking the camera is your best friend."

⋐⋑⋐⋑

Thin Veil

Fall 1966—Sunday Night

Dear Jay,

It was so good to have you here for the weekend. As always we seem to be caught up with other people. In our concern for them and their reactions to our decisions, we find ourselves doing things for their "pleased understanding," rather than following our own desires.

I wish you could have been with us more—but by so doing I'm sure you would have—due to the circumstances—hurt Hellie and Jack—and so it goes. There must be some way of meeting obligations without short-circuiting one's own wishes—but as yet, I have not found the solution.

Jay, I know your indecision about the future is a constant mental, emotional concern. But I'm just as sure what you're doing is right for now and the future. There is no way of evaluating the worth of time spent, but there has rarely been a time in history when mankind—should say Western Man—and through him the world—was so in need of moral, religious and political leadership. The three terms—moral, religious, political—are so intertwined they are inseparable in the sense I use the words. What you are learning now is a resource for the future and the foundation on which your contribution to life and God will be based.

When you left today, I understood so totally how you felt—and I felt exactly the same way. The feeling has come over me often now and in the past—leaving my father, Grinnell and Grandmother—Mother, Pat, and yourself to go to sea—any parting. One knows he must live his own life—but where love has strong bonds—any leaving of the physical presence of those we love is a shock momentarily.

There is a poem "Mizpah" which states the reality well. I don't have my reference books here so I can't quote it. Grandmother has it framed and hanging on her bedroom wall. A line which is the theme says "only a thin veil hangs between the places where we are." This is true—for I feel you are with me always and I hope you know how I am always with you.

Your future is bright indeed. Be patient. Don't press. Time will give you the insight to know what is best for you in your contribution to this world—and it will be a great contribution because of your depth of knowledge (which you're gaining each day) and your sincere desire to help others.

Mom and I love you and Betty so much. I know we can be together more in the days ahead and we look forward to it.

All my love, always,
Dad

In parting from Mom and Dad that Sunday in Washington to return to ETS, I had suddenly burst into tears. It was the first time I had cried since leaving home for Duke. Once more Dad reminded me that although we were apart physically, we were always close spiritually. His comforting words—"I feel you are with me always and I hope you know how I am always with you"—were similar to those conveyed to a lonesome, homesick young man six years before.

The poem to which Dad referred, "Mizpah" by Julia Baker, is based on the Mizpah Benediction of Genesis. In reads, in part:

Go thou thy way, and I go mine,
Apart, yet not afar;
Only a thin veil hangs between
The pathways where we are.

And God keep watch 'tween thee and me
This is my prayer,
He looks thy way, He looketh mine,
And keeps us near.

I sigh sometimes to see thy face,
But since this may not be,
I'll leave thee to the care of Him,
Who cares for thee and me.

And though our paths be separate,
And thy way is not mine,
Yet coming to the Mercy seat,
My soul will meet with thine.

And "God keep watch 'tween thee and me,"
I'll whisper there.
He blesseth thee, He blesseth me,
And in this we are near.

Indeed, I was uplifted and sustained by his words of love and encouragement in these sometimes lonely and difficult years, and I came to realize how true were the words of that poem: only a thin veil hung between the places where we were, and I felt that he was with me, and I with him, always.

Postscript

My father's letters of encouragement and love and my reflections on them cover six years in the 1960s. They were deeply important to me then and remain so now, although by no means do they represent the sum total of correspondence and communication between us. On the contrary, as life continued to pull us in different directions, frequently rewarding yet sometimes challenging, Dad remained a constant source of optimism, understanding, and support. I hope that as I grew older and wiser and my own experiences broadened, I was able to return the favor.

As in most families, our lives were filled at times with complexities, heartache, and ambiguities, but for my father, mother, brother, and me, the years following these letters were also abundant with happiness, laughter, joy, and contentment.

The life of a football coach is never an easy one. Mary Wilkinson was the consummate role model when it came to supporting a coaching husband. And when Dad's aspirations turned toward holding public office, she assumed her new role as "running mate" with great charm, total class, and immense popularity on the campaign trail. My parents continued to travel domestically and internationally through the mid-70s, but time spent apart over so many years ultimately took its toll on their relationship, and they were divorced in 1975 after thirty-seven years of marriage. The transition was difficult for her—and tough on her grown sons— since her life had revolved around her beloved family. But after a time of mourning and adjustment, she rallied to take on her new circumstances with courage and determination.

When Mom decided to take cooking classes in France, to prepare for that adventure she enrolled in a French language course at Oklahoma City University. Once comfortable with the vernacular, she was off to Europe, ultimately learning the finer points of preparing and serving French cuisine via a program in which students watched, learned, practiced, and perfected their craft in the kitchens of individual homes. The experience enhanced her reputation as the consummate hostess whose dinner parties were known for both gourmet meals and lively conversation.

Naturally shy by nature, Mom grew more comfortable and confident as she aged. At age sixty-two, still a striking presence at five feet, six inches tall and 116 pounds and now with a head of brilliant white hair, she mustered the courage to audition at a local modeling agency. Given her special grace, dignity, and beauty, and the fact that she was still comfortable in three-inch heels, she became an immediate hit on the runway. I swelled with pride at seeing her beaming smile as she dazzled audiences in elegant designer clothing.

A lifelong avid reader, Mom applied to became a part-time clerk at Full Circle Bookstore in Oklahoma City. The job required her to master new skills, most notably the computerized cash register, and as always she rose to the task. She enjoyed the job immensely, falling in love with her co-workers, customers, and books. She was especially adept at offering twenty-second book reviews for the store's delighted patrons.

Books were by no means her only escape, and indeed she may

have been more active in "retirement" than as a younger woman. She continued to travel throughout the world and kept a diary of pictures and postcards from her favorite destinations—China, Australia, Europe, and Central America. She loved sharing those scrapbooks, and when she could no longer travel, her mementos became a way to relive the thrill of her adventures.

After a series of strokes, Mom moved to the Waterford assisted living facility in Oklahoma City. She soon adapted to her new surroundings, expanded her circle of friends, and became a regular in the parlor, playing bridge. Our initial concerns notwithstanding, she thrived there for some seven years. Then one spring day, after driving to the mall to pick up Easter cards for her grandchildren, she slipped and fell and broke her hip. She developed pneumonia and died less than a month later, on April 24, 2005, two months away from celebrating her eighty-ninth birthday. Mom was active to the end and sharp as a tack, and all of her family had a chance to say good-bye.

My brother Pat is a distinguished and respected national and international leader in the field of retinal ophthalmology. After receiving his medical degree from Johns Hopkins University in 1965, he was an intern and resident there for the following four years. He then received fellowship training in vitreoretinal diseases at the University of Miami and subsequently joined the faculty at the University of Oklahoma, where he was a clinical professor of ophthalmology for more than fifteen years.

Pat was always an excellent student and his work ethic and genuine concern for his patients contributed to his career. Since 1992 he has served as chair of the Department of Ophthalmology at the Greater Baltimore Medical Center and as a professor in the Department of Ophthalmology at Johns Hopkins. In addition, he has served as a director and chair of the American Board of Ophthalmology and as president of the American Academy of

Ophthalmology and American Ophthalmological Society. He has published extensively on a variety of subjects.

Besides his expertise in retina surgery, Pat has been affiliated with teaching hospitals throughout his medical career and has considered the aspect of training to be one of his proudest achievements. Clearly, he too was influenced by Dad's core principles. Pat's daughters—Laura Gabel, a registered nurse, and Melinda Lee, a publicist with Neiman Marcus—are both married and have one child each. Since 1992 Pat has been married to the former Alice Michels, and he has two step-children and three step-grandchildren.

Although ordained to the deaconate following graduation from ETS, I made a final decision in 1968 not to enter the priesthood. The decision resulted from an inner dialogue best described as a tug of war. One the one hand, I had enormous respect for the clergy ministering to a particular community of church members in their joys and sorrows, their life and death circumstances, which I saw in my part-time role at St. John's Episcopal Church. On the other hand, I had been influenced by working in the slums of Boston, in a geriatrics ward, and then for Governor Dewey Bartlett, all of which helped inspire me to aim for a life of public service.

I was caught up in what I called the "Kennedy idealism," wanting to be involved on a wider scale, undertaking an active role in state and national government to make our country and world better. Our ETS dean John Coburn stressed that God cares less about whether you get ordained than about whether you are responding to him in your life situation. I hoped that by trying to help others through public service, I was being honest to God and my faith commitments.

After my failed bid for Congress I decided to enter business and spent thirty-seven years in executive management with four different companies specializing in employer-sponsored retirement plans. First I joined Planned Marketing Associates in Dallas, Texas, and like the seventh-team quarterback of my sophomore year at Duke, I had to work my way up the ladder; through preparation, attitude, and perseverance, I eventually became vice president of account development.

Later I joined Public Employees Benefit Services Corporation (PEBSCO) and became president of the company when it was sold to Nationwide Insurance. During the next fifteen years PEBSCO (now Nationwide Retirement Solutions) grew to become the nation's largest manager of public-sector defined-contribution plans. In that time the number of PEBSCO political subdivisions sponsoring employee programs increased from zero to six thousand, while assets grew from $300 million to more than $30 billion. Once again, principles learned from my father influenced my approach as I led our company from its infancy to becoming the leader with the dominant market share in the industry. I was proud that we had one of the most close-knit organizations in the country with superb morale, discipline, and service.

I then joined Invesco, a $400 billion investment management firm in Atlanta, Georgia, as senior vice president and eventual global partner. There I was responsible for bank, insurance company, broker/dealer, and third-party relationships. And later I moved on to Houston, Texas, to become executive vice president for Variable Annuity Life Insurance Company (VALIC), a $60 billion life insurance retirement company, where I led a team engaged in the acquisition and retention of large institutional groups in the higher education, health care, government, and k–12 markets.

In 1979 I was inducted into the Duke University Sports Hall of Fame; in 1989 I was among six individuals to receive the NCAA Silver Anniversary Award, given annually in recognition of business and civic leadership twenty-five years after graduation; and recently I was recognized by the Atlantic Coast Conference as a member of the 2010 Class of Football Legends.

My first wife Betty and I had two wonderful daughters, who are grown now with families of their own. Kirsten and her husband David Griffin have a daughter and two sons. Holly and her husband Jim Parmelee have twin boys and another son. I remarried in 1977 to Rita Davis of Louisville, Kentucky, and we have a son, P.J., and a daughter, Julie. P.J. and his wife Maegan have one son.

While I consider myself semi-retired, I have enjoyed being involved in motivational talks to groups around the country centered on the principles in this book.

Dad was a key figure in the administrations of several presidents. In addition to his work with President Kennedy's Council on Physical Fitness, he became a special consultant during President Nixon's first administration, where for two years he was an adviser on the substantive issues of drug abuse, youth affairs, and volunteerism. President Ford appointed Dad to the United States Commission of Olympic Sports, and President Reagan appointed him to the Board of Visitors of the United States Air Force Academy. He also was a state chair for George H. W. Bush's successful presidential campaign and was a close friend to the nation's forty-first chief executive.

After leaving the University of Oklahoma, Dad served as a respected sports television commentator for twenty years, working on the network level at NBC, ABC, and ESPN, with notable broadcasters such as Jim Simpson, Chris Schenkel, and Keith Jackson. He remained active in the Coach-of-the-Year clinics with Duffy Daugherty until the late 1980s and chaired two successful companies, Planned Marketing Associates and PEBSCO, both corporate leaders in the retirement services industry.

He spent the last eighteen years of his life with his second wife,

Donna O'Donnohue, whom he married in 1976. Two years later he accepted the position of head football coach of the St. Louis Cardinals. As a result, he and Donna moved to St. Louis, where they continued to live after he was fired as coach of the Cardinals following his second year of coaching. He became president of the United States Gymnastics Federation, and under his watch the U.S. men captured team gold and the women took team silver at the 1984 Olympic Games in Los Angeles.

Dad was elected to the Oklahoma Hall of Fame in 1963, the College Football Hall of Fame in 1969, and the Oklahoma Sports Hall of Fame in 1986 and is also a member of the University of Minnesota Athletics Hall of Fame. *Sporting News* lists him as one of the fifty greatest coaches of all time, *Sports Illustrated* ranks his 1953–57 Oklahoma teams among the ten greatest sports dynasties of the twentieth century, and ESPN rates his 1956 Sooners as one of the top ten college football teams in history.

He developed congestive heart failure in 1986 and later suffered a series of strokes that impaired his eyesight and affected his memory. During his last two weeks Pat and I both spent quiet time with him at his home. He died peacefully on February 9, 1994. I am so very proud that he was my father and always remain grateful for his loving support to me, our family, and so many others.

Acknowledgments

Many people have contributed to the final form of this book, and I want to offer my gratitude and appreciation to them all.

Nancy Swanson Pedden was really its architect. She pleaded for my father's letters to be shared and persuaded me to add background and commentary on them. Throughout the initial assembling of the manuscript she was a tireless helper and offered numerous constructive suggestions.

Tim Gregg's professional skills were of enormous value. He convinced me to broaden the story by addressing more fully what was happening in my life at the time, so as to convey what the letters meant to me when they arrived and how meaningful they remain today. He thus made substantive contributions regarding the organization, themes, and flow of the narrative as a whole. Tim has been an invaluable contributor to my motivational speaking and also created my website (www.winningthewilkinsonway.com).

Jay Dew, acquisitions editor at the University of Oklahoma Press, played a key role during the gestation period. His confidence that the project had merit was validating to me, and his guidance, patience, and understanding helped make the book a reality. Manuscript editor Emily Jerman and copy editor Sally

Antrobus, through their attention to detail, greatly strengthened the text and presentation during the final stages of development and production.

From the inception to the conclusion of the project, my brother Pat provided thoughtful advice and useful thematic ideas. Likewise enthusiastic and offering many suggestions were my children and their spouses—Kirsten and David Griffin, Holly and Jim Parmelee, P. J. and Maegan Wilkinson, and Julie Wilkinson—and cousins Mary Mistler and Jack Ransom. Many other people were instrumental in their support and confirmation, and in particular I thank Bill Carmack, John David Davenport, Chuck Bowman, Mary Dinkins, George H. Parker III, Kevin White, C. G. Newsome, Rhonda Henry, Dan Rupp, Carmen Scarpa, Bill Futrell, Clint Davidson, Sue Wasiolek, Joe Castiglione, and Gerald Wilson for their encouragement and advice.

And heartfelt thanks go to my wife Rita, who consistently affirmed the importance of the book and gave encouragement, love, and support throughout the entire process.